EDINBURGH WALKS

Volume One

CAMPBELL BROWN & STEVEN WIGGINS

Maps *Simon Manfield*
Illustrations *Don Allan*
Photographs *Steven Wiggins*

First Published 1989
by B+W Publishing
Edinburgh
Revised Edition 1990
Printed in Scotland
at Meigle Printers Ltd
Galashiels
© Campbell Brown & Steven Wiggins
ISBN 0 951515 0 1

Other titles available

Edinburgh Walks Volume Two

The Pentlands and the Lothians

ISBN 0 951515 3 6

Glasgow Walks

ISBN 0 951515 1 X

B+W Publishing 7 Sciennes Edinburgh EH9 1NH

Contents

16 Pages of Photographs between pages 40 & 41

Authors Note

Throughout the text you will find a series of numbers. These relate directly to the numbers on the maps and will enable you to see at a glance exactly where the information relevant to any point of interest on the walk is to be found.

For those walks away from the city centre, a general location map has been included, together with public transport details. All buses mentioned in the text are Lothian Regon Transport (maroon & white).

Acknowledgements
We would like to thank:
The Desktop Publishing Centre (031-558 3136)
The Graphics Company (031-557 8675)
James Robertson
George Sassoon for *The General* by Siegfried Sassoon

b+w

INTRODUCTION

Edinburgh is a city that demands to be walked in. Although, in Robert Louis Stevenson's phrase, a precipitious city, any exertion in exploring its peaks and depths is usually well rewarded, whether by marvellous views or the pleasure of discovering an unexpected architectural quirk or historical feature. It is a place with an anecdote on every corner, and this guide excels in picking out those oddities and inscriptions that are easily missed or which are not always self-explanatory. Natives of Edinburgh will be familiar with some but not all of these. Visitors will find these walks a fine antidote to the patchy, inaccurate blurbs of larger travel guides which seem often to assume a collective tourist I.Q. so miniscule as to be incapable of appreciating anything less obvious than the Castle and the Palace of Holyrood.

Sir Walter Scott, Edinburgh's most famous son, whose memory is preserved everywhere in the names of pubs and clubs, to say nothing of a football team, a railway station and the largest monument ever built to celebrate a literary figure, recorded much of the story of Edinburgh in his novels poems and histories. I would defy anyone with an imagination to read the first few chapters of *The Heart of Midlothian*, describing the Porteous Riots, and then be able to walk through the Grassmarket and the closes of the Old Town without feeling the breath of the past on their neck. The past and the present mingle easily in this town because its centre is still lived in - by night and by day; and an unpretentious, informative book like this will play its part in making people aware of the relationship between the old and the new, and thus will help to create a popular defence against attempts (which will surely be made) by P.R. bandits, heritage-floggers and the makers of costume-drama tourist traps to turn Edinburgh into a pseudo-historic toy-town. May that day never arrive! And may people enjoy this city and its walks, as they are presented here in this most welcome guide, for many years to come.

Dr James Robertson
Edinburgh 1990

I
The Royal Mile
The Castle to St Giles Cathedral

Edinburgh Castle
Earl Haig
Camera Obscura
Gladstone's Land
Deacon Brodie
Tolbooth Site
St Giles Cathedral

Starting Point: *THE CASTLE ESPLANADE*

RECOMMENDED CAFES & BARS
The Jolly Judge, 7 James Court
The Lower Aisle Restaurant, St Giles Cathedral
Le Sept, 7 Old Fishmarket Close (past St Giles)

EDINBURGH CASTLE (I) is one of the world's most striking landmarks, sitting high up on Castle Hill and visible from all over the city. Its history is too rich and varied to be covered fully here, as its buildings vary in age and style from the Norman chapel of St Margaret to the National War Memorial dating from the end of the First World War. Some of the monuments on the Castle Esplanade are of special interest, including those commemorating Earl Haig, Commander of the British Army on the Western Front in World War One, who was born in this city (see New Town walk), and Ensign Ewart of the Scots Greys who captured the French 45th Regiment's colours at the battle of Waterloo in 1815. The Castle is open Mon-Sat 9.30-5pm, Sun 11-5pm. Entry £2.20.

From the Castle, walk down Castle Hill, past Cannonball House on the right. Immediately on the left is the Outlook Tower or **Camera Obscura (2),** *and on the right the Scottish Whisky Heritage Centre. Continue along the Lawnmarket until you reach* **Gladstones Land (3),** *just after James' Court, on the left.*

GLADSTONE'S LAND is an excellent example of a Land, or block of flats, which was bought by Thomas Gledstanes, a merchant, in 1617. It was built high and narrow as a result of the lack of space in the crowded walled Old Town. The Land has been restored by the National Trust for Scotland and is open to the public from April 1 to October 31 (Mon-Sat 10am-5pm; Sun 2pm-5pm, entry £1.50). Almost as old as Gladstone's Land is Lady Stair's House, built around 1622. Accessible through Lady Stair's Close, the house is now a museum dedicated to Robert Burns, Robert Louis Stevenson and Sir Walter Scott. On the other side of the Lawnmarket, just before George IV Bridge, is **Brodie's Close (4).**

DEACON WILLIAM BRODIE lived here until his execution in October 1788. He had been one of the city's most respected citizens, who for many years combined a secret life of crime with a blameless public life. A man of great character and style, his private life was hampered by large gambling debts and the need to support his mistresses and illegitimate children, so he took to burglary by night. At his trial, Brodie appeared dressed entirely in black silk and behaved impeccably. The final irony of Brodie's life was that he himself had invented the drop on the gallows that took him so efficiently into oblivion. He is said to have died with a wry smile on his face, and his story apparently inspired **Robert Louis Stevenson** to write *Dr Jekyll and Mr Hyde.*

Cross George IV Bridge at the traffic lights and walk down to **Parliament Square (5).**

PARLIAMENT SQUARE is situated opposite St Giles Street, (which was built in the 1860's to provide offices for newspapers such as *The Edinburgh Courant, The Daily Review* and *The Glasgow Herald*). Paradoxically, its history is dominated by a building that is no longer present, the Tolbooth, and the site of this ancient building is marked out by brass setts

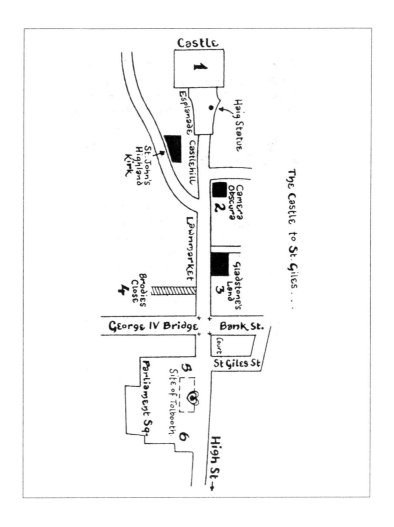

The Castle to St. Giles . . .

Castle
1

Esplanade Castlehill

Haig Statue

St. John's Highland Kirk

Camera Obscura
2

Lawnmarket

Gladstone's Land
3

Brodies Close
4

George IV Bridge

Bank St.

Court

St Giles St

5
Site of Tolbooth
6

Parliament Sq.

High St →

3

After all, I reflected I was like my neighbours; and then I smiled, comparing myself with other men, comparing my active goodwill with the lazy cruelty of their neglect. And at the very moment of that vainglorious thought, a qualm came over me, a horrid nausea and the most deadly shuddering. These passed away, and left me faint; and then in its turn the faintness subsided, I began to be aware of a change in the temper of my thoughts, a greater boldness, a contempt of danger, a solution of the bonds of obligation. I looked down; my clothes hung formlessly on my shrunken limbs; the hand that lay on my knee was corded and hairy. I was once more Edward Hyde. A moment before I had been safe of all men's respect, wealthy, beloved- the cloth laying for me in the dining room at home; and now I was the common quarry of mankind, hunted, houseless, a known murderer, thrall to the gallows.

Dr Jekyll and Mr Hyde by **R L Stevenson**

inlaid into the square. Sir Walter Scott described the Tolbooth, which was initially the place to pay taxes and later the town prison and place of execution, as *The Heart Of Midlothian,* and a heart shaped device marks the site of the main door. The Tolbooth existed from early times and in 1438 was used as a Parliament building to deliberate on matters arising from the assassination of James I. By 1817 the building had been demolished and a new jail built on Calton Hill. Interestingly, the gateway, door and padlock of the Tolbooth were transferred to Sir Walter Scott's house at Abbotsford in the Borders near Galashiels. The Tolbooth features in much of Edinburgh's history, the **Deacon Brodie** case, the escape from prison of a youth called Hay (who hid in Bloody MacKenzies mausoleum in Greyfriars Kirkyard for six weeks), and the **Porteous Riots** (see Grassmarket/ Greyfriars walk). It was immortalised in Scott's novel *The Heart of Midlothian:* "They eagerly relieved each other at the labour of assailing the Tolbooth door: yet such was its strength, that it denied their efforts. At length, a voice was heard to pronounce the words, "Try it with fire"...A huge red glaring bonfire speedily arose close to the door of the prison, sending up a tall column of smoke and flame against its antique turrets and strongly-grated windows..."

Dominating Parliament Square is **St Giles Cathedral (6).**

ST GILES CATHEDRAL'S most distinctive external feature is the Crown Tower of 1495. The Cathedral itself was originally dedicated to St Giles by the Bishop of St Andrews in 1243, although there has been a church on this site since at least 850. The oldest parts of the present structure date from 1120, and it was much enlarged in the years between 1385 and 1520. The Cathedral contains many monuments to well-known figures from Scottish history, the two most elaborate being those to the 1st Marquis of Argyll and his arch enemy the Marquis of Montrose.

Enter the Cathedral by the main door from Parliament Square.

Immediately to the left is the **ALBANY AISLE**, founded in 1400 and at present the site of several war memorials including a distinctive French one, dating from 1951, which commemorates Scottish soldiers killed in World War I.

Continue up three steps, past memorial plaques to those killed in the long-forgotten colonial campaigns of the 19th century, to the statue of **JOHN KNOX**, who was buried nearby in 1572. Knox was the leading figure in the Scottish Reformation, whose career as a reformer began at St Andrews University under the influence of George Wishart. After his mentor was burnt at the stake for his heretical views in 1546 on the orders of Cardinal Beaton, Knox's involvement with those who subsequently assasinated Beaton led to two years as a prisoner in a French galley. He later spent six years in Geneva where he was greatly influenced by the teachings of **Calvin**.

Knox returned to Scotland in 1559 and spent the rest of his life struggling to ensure the survival of the Reformation in Scotland. His best known literary work was the quaintly titled *First Blast Of The Trumpet Against The Monstrous Regiment Of Women*.

Just past the statue of Knox, in an alcove on the left, is the memorial to Archibald Campbell, 8th Earl and 1st Marquis of Argyll (1607-1661). **'Cross-eyed Archibald'** as he was known, led the more radical Covenanters against Charles I, but came to terms with Charles II, whom he crowned at Scone in January 1651. But his association with the Cromwellian Administration led to his downfall, and he was executed when Charles II returned in 1661 (see Grassmarket/Greyfriars walk). The bitter inscription above the reclining figure of Argyll is:

**I set the crown on the King's head,
He hastens me to a better crown than his own.**

Moving on down the left hand side of the Cathedral, you will see more memorials to the victims of World War I. Continue on across the sanctuary to the right hand side of the Cathedral. You are now facing back towards the main door, and immediately on your left is the **ROYAL PEW**, the stalls used by Queen Elizabeth II and the Duke of Edinburgh.

In an alcove a little further down this side of the Cathedral, is the

monument to James Graham, **1st MARQUIS OF MONTROSE** (1612-1650), the soldier and poet, who was hanged outside the Cathedral on 21st May 1650. Montrose fought for Charles I in the civil war, before being defeated near Selkirk in 1645 and fleeing abroad. Returning in 1650 to lead another Royalist Uprising, he was defeated at Carbisdale in Sutherland, taken prisoner at Ardvreck Castle on Loch Assynt and finally executed in Edinburgh. His elaborate monument is inscribed with verses he composed the night before his execution:

> **Scatter my ashes, strew them in the air,**
> **Lord since thou knowest where all these atoms are,**
> **I'm hopeful thou'lt recover once my dust,**
> **And confident thou'lt raise me with the just.**

Just before you reach the main door on the way out, there is a large bronze memorial plaque to **Robert Louis Stevenson** which was designed by

Augustus St Gaudens in 1904. Directly above the main door is a fine contemporary stained-glass window to the memory of **Robert Burns**.

The Cathedral holds services at 10am and 11.30am on Sundays, and at 12 noon on weekdays. There is also a shop and an excellent restaurant, **'The Lower Aisle'**, which is open from 10am to 4.30pm.

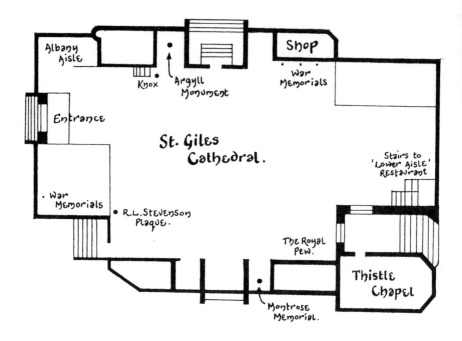

2
The Royal Mile
Tron Kirk to Holyrood

Tron Kirk
Paisley Close
John Knox House
Huntley House Museum
Robert Burns
Holyroodhouse Palace

Starting Point: **THE TRON KIRK (1)**
Just before the traffic lights at the junction between
the High Street and the North and South Bridges

RECOMMENDED CAFES & BARS
The Fudge House, 197 Canongate
Clarinda's Tearoom, 69 Canongate
Abbey Strand Tearoom, Holyrood

THE TRON KIRK was founded in 1637 to cater for the needs of the expanding congregation of St Giles Cathedral. The name came from the old public weigh beam, the 'Salt Tron', which stood nearby. The church was designed by John Mylne and is notable for its unusual latticed truss roof construction. The design seems to have been influenced by continental churches, in particular those of the Netherlands and Denmark. Some parts of the Tron were removed in 1785 to make way for better access to the North and South Bridges, and the old steeple was destroyed in the great fire of 1824. The Tron closed as a place of worship in 1952, and is now the site of archaeological excavations, which have uncovered the remains of the streets that previously stood on this site. Regular exhibitions about the

Old Town are also held here.

Cross over the Bridges and walk down the High Street to Paisley Close.

PAISLEY CLOSE is on the left of the High Street, and at its entrance is the finely executed carving of a young boy's head by John Rhind. This marks the site of a nineteenth century tenement collapse that killed around thirty people. When rescuers arrived they heard a voice cry out from the rubble "Heave awa' chaps, I'm no dead yet!". The boy was pulled alive from the fallen masonry and the inscription and carving are a reminder of his fortunate escape.

Continuing down the hill, John Knox's house is on the left (open Mon-Sat 10am-5pm, entry £1), and on the right directly opposite is the **Museum of Childhood** (Mon-Sat 10am-5pm, entry free). Also on the right is **World's End Close**, which for many years marked the eastern extremity of the old city. Many culprits were whipped through the town after being stripped at the Stripping Close (now demolished) near the castle, and this brutal ceremony always ended at World's End Close.

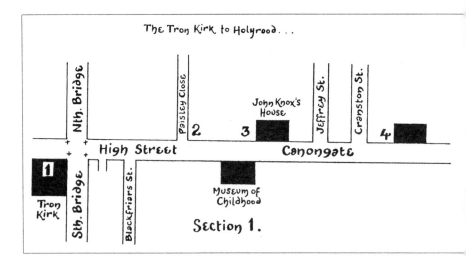

The Tron Kirk to Holyrood . . .

Section 1.

Continue on past the traffic lights at the junction of Jeffrey Street and if you look high up on the wall above the grocer's shop on the left you will see a Moorish carved figure. This marks the site of
MOROCCO'S LAND (4).

There are several apocryphal stories relating to this unlikely figure, but perhaps the most interesting is that of a young man who fled from the city in disgrace and ended up in Morocco. He made his fortune there and became determined to take his revenge upon the city. He returned with a small fleet and landed in Edinburgh with a force of Moorish soldiers. But he was deflected from his original purpose and eventually gained the gratitude of the city by saving the life of the Provost's daughter, whom he later married. He became Provost himself in due course and built the house known as Morocco's Land. The carved figure was his acknowledgement of the source of his good fortune. The reality behind the carving is doubtless more prosaic than this romantic story. The building that now stands on this site is a replica of an 18th century tenement which stood close by. The carved figure is all that remains of this earlier building.

Carry on down the Canongate until you reach the Canongate Tolbooth

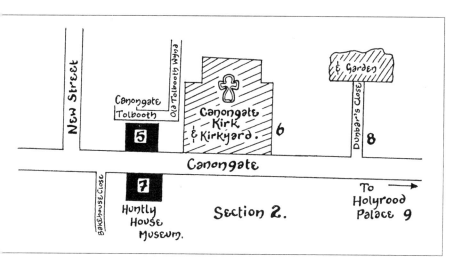

with its prominent clock, just after Tolbooth Wynd. Built in 1591, this is where the town council met, and was also the local courtroom. It now houses a permanent exhibition. Just past the Tolbooth is the **Canongate Kirk (6),** *in the shadow of the former Royal High School on Regent Road.*

THE CANONGATE KIRK was built between 1688 and 1690. The Kirk itself has a curious facade, crowned with a set of antlers - the emblem of the Canongate. The kirkyard is of particular interest, as it contains the graves of Adam Smith, author of *The Wealth of Nations*, and Robert Fergusson (1751-1774) the poet, who died in a lunatic asylum at the age of 23.

Adam Smith (1723-1790) took 12 years to write his magnum opus *An Inquiry into the Nature and Causes of the Wealth of Nations*, and probably about the same time in research before that, but finally published on the 9th March 1776 to critical acclaim. The book is still highly influencial more than 200 years later. He was a very sociable man whose door was always open to visitors, and it was during one of his regular Sunday gatherings in 1790 that he spoke the words: "I believe we must adjourn this meeting, gentlemen, to some other place." He died shortly afterwards.

The inscription on Robert Fergusson's tombstone was written by Robert Burns.

> **No sculptured Marble here nor pompous lay**
> **No storied Urn nor animated Bust**
> **This simple Stone directs Pale Scotia's way**
> **To pour her Sorrows o'er her Poet's Dust**

Robert Louis Stevenson intended to restore the memorial after it fell into disrepair in the 19th century, but died before he could do so. Part of what Stevenson would have put on the restored stone was the simple message: "from one Edinburgh lad to another".

On the other side of the road is **Huntly House Museum (7).**

HUNTLY HOUSE MUSEUM is one of the best places to investigate

John Knox House

the local history of Edinburgh. It is a beautifully preserved 16th century building, and in the 18th century was the headquarters of one of the city's powerful guilds, the Hammermen, or Smiths. The interior is a series of small rooms housing collections of Roman artefacts, historic documents, silverware, glassware, pottery, shop signs and other objects gathered from local industries. The establishment of a museum here in 1924 put an end to the century of neglect suffered by this area after the building of the New Town. Also in the collections are the collar and dinner dish of **Greyfriars Bobby** and some of the personal belongings of **Earl Haig.** (Open 10am-5pm in winter, 10am-6pm in summer & 2-5pm Sun during festival).

Across the road is **DUNBAR'S CLOSE (8)**, a reconstruction of a typical 17th century garden which displays many of the features of formal gardens of the time, including cropped box hedges. From the back of the garden there is a good view of the Burns Memorial.

Continuing down the Canongate, this walk ends at the **PALACE OF HOLYROODHOUSE (9)**, the offical residence of the Queen in Scotland. Mary Queen of Scots came here in 1561 on her return from France, and lived here for six eventful years. Her secretary David Rizzio was murdered in the Palace by Lord Darnley, her husband, and his associates. Holyrood is open to the public (9.30am-5.15pm in summer (Sun 10.30-4.30pm); 9.30-3.45pm in winter; entry £1.50).

This is the end of the second Old Town walk, but can be followed by the Holyrood Park walk, which offers superb views of both the Palace and the city.

3
The New Town

Europe's Finest Georgian Architecture
The Scottish National Portrait Gallery
The Georgian House
David Hume
Sir Walter Scott
Earl Haig
Alexander Graham Bell

Starting Point: **ROYAL BANK OF SCOTLAND (1)**
on the east side of St Andrew Square

RECOMMENDED CAFES & BARS
Laigh Kitchen, 121 Hanover Street
(Reconstructed c18th Tearoom)
Boxers, 18 Howe Street
Whighams, 13 Hope Street
Bianco's, 9/11 Hope Street

Before the Nor' Loch was drained, it was a major deterrent to anyone thinking of attacking the castle. It stood roughly where Princes St Gardens are today, in a trench gouged out by a glacial ice flow, and the loch left the area where the centre of the New Town now stands virtually cut off from the Old Town. As the stagnant water was being drained, the New Town was being built. This was the time of the Scottish Enlightenment and the start of Edinburgh's Golden Age, sponsored by people like the philosopher David Hume, Sir Henry Raeburn and Sir Walter Scott. An early exercise in town planning, the New Town design was chosen through a competition, won in 1767 by a 23 year old architect, James Craig. His plan was well suited to the site, and incorporated two large open squares, one at each end of a gridiron. The Georgian developments continued from 1767 to 1840, and now form one of the largest conservation areas in Europe. As each phase of the work was undertaken, the pattern was extended to the north, and expanded in terms of the buildings themselves and the extravagance of the spaces in between. Craig's work on George Street, St Andrew Square and Charlotte Square was followed by that of William Sibbald and Robert Reid who designed and built Great King Street, parallel to George Street, and Drummond Place and Royal Circus to mirror the central squares. James Gillespie Graham designed the third phase which includes the magnificent Moray Place and Ainslie Place.

Inside the **ROYAL BANK (1)** is a superb starry dome. Formerly the townhouse of Sir Lawrence Dundas, the building was bought by the bank in the mid 19th century and modified for their purposes. It was at this time that the dome was added. James Craig's original plan for the New Town included a church at each end of George Street, but this never materialised. Instead, a townhouse was built for Sir Lawrence and St Andrew's and St George's Church, originally planned for the site, was moved to George Street.

THE MELVILLE MONUMENT (2) of 1823 is in the centre of St. Andrew Square and commemorates the 1st Viscount Melville, Henry Dundas (1742-1811). He was a major political figure of his time, and in a career that spanned forty years was Home Secretary, Secretary of State for War, Lord Advocate of Scotland, and a close friend of William Pitt. However, his career was abruptly terminated as the result of a financial scandal during his time as treasurer of the Navy.

On the far side of the square, **DAVID HUME** the philosopher built his town house on the corner of South St David Street and St Andrew Square. Although born in Edinburgh in 1711, he lived in the country until the age of 40 when he bought a small house on the Canongate, a rather second rate residence according to Robert Chambers. This was after the publication of his first major philosophical work in 1738, *A Treatise on Human Nature,*

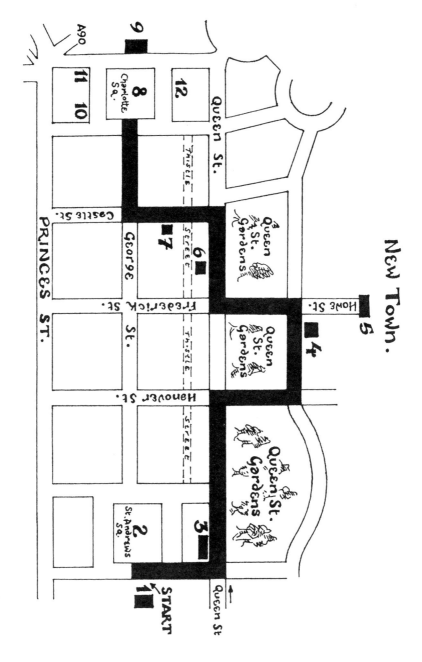

New Town.

9
A90
11 10
Charlotte Sq.
8
12
Queen St.

Thistle

Castle St.
George
7
6
Queen St. Gardens

Street
PRINCES ST.
Frederick St.
Howe St.
5
Street

Thistle
St.
4
Queen St. Gardens

Hanover St.
Street

Thistle
St. Andrews Sq.
2
Street
3
Queen St. Gardens
Queen St

START
1

17

which established his reputation. All his life he devoted himself entirely to the study of philosophy: "I found an insurmountable aversion to everything but the pursuits of philosophy and general learning. I resolved to make a very rigid frugality supply my deficiency of fortune, to maintain unimpaired my independency, and to regard every object as contemptible, except the improvement of my talents in literature." Hume published his *Political Discourses* in 1852, where he dealt with the subjects of commerce, money and the balance of trade. It was another best seller. He later moved to Paris as Secretary to the Earl of Hertford, and after that became an Under Secretary of State and moved back to Edinburgh. He built his New Town house in 1771, and died there in 1776.

> **"It is difficult for a man to speak long**
> **of himself without vanity"**
> David Hume

Walk north from St Andrew Square, past the bus station on the right, and down North St Andrew Street. Turn left at the bottom and the first building on the left is **The National Portrait Gallery (3).**

THE SCOTTISH NATIONAL PORTRAIT GALLERY on Queen Street is one of Scotland's finest galleries. Neo-Gothic in design, and with a superb exterior, this red sandstone structure was built in the 1880's with money donated by John Ritchie Finlay, the philanthropic owner of *The Scotsman* newspaper. Portraits of famous Scots to be found here include: **Mary Queen of Scots** (the macabre split picture of whom becomes a skull when viewed from an angle), **Bonnie Prince Charlie, Sir Walter Scott, The Queen Mother, Lord Home,** and **Sean Connery.** There is also an extensive collection of Scottish photography by pioneers such as Hill and Adamson, as well as The Roman Room and the archaeological collection. The building also houses a guillotine called **'The Maiden'**, which was used between 1565 and 1710. This machine replaced beheading by sword as the accepted form of aristocratic execution, but Scotland stopped using it 80 years before the French Revolution saw its return to widespread use in the Terror of 1793. (Open 10am-5pm; Sun 2-5pm; entry free)

Continue along Queen Street and turn right into Queen Street Gardens East. Queen Street Gardens form a natural break between the first and second phases of New Town development. Turn left into Heriot Row, and No.17 was the home of **Robert Louis Stevenson (4)**, *and a little further on No.31 was the home of James Clerk Maxwell (see Stockbridge walk).*

ROBERT LOUIS STEVENSON is best remembered for his novels *Dr Jekyll and Mr Hyde, Treasure Island,* and *Kidnapped,* as well as *A Childs Garden of Verses.* Some information about his life can be found at the Gardens opposite the house. Above the front door there is a model of a lighthouse in the window, a reminder of the fact that the Stevenson family were well known lighthouse engineers and builders. Stevenson never really enjoyed good health, and spent many hours in the house looking out over the Gardens as he wrote. He eventually left the damp Edinburgh climate for France, where he married the American Fanny Osbourne and later found much better weather in Tahiti, Hawaii and finally Samoa where he died in 1894. He wrote his own epitaph for his grave at Mount Vaea which included the immortal words "home is the sailor, home from the sea, and the hunter home from the hill."

> **"I remember him as if it were yesterday, as he came plodding to the inn door, his sea-chest following behind him in a hand barrow; a tall, strong, heavy, nut-brown man; his tarry pigtail falling over the shoulders of his soiled blue coat; his hands ragged and scarred, with black, broken nails; and the sabre cut across one cheek, a dirty, livid white. I remember him looking around the cove and whistling to himself as he did so, and then breaking out in that old sea-song that he sang so often afterwards: 'Fifteen men on the dead man's chest, Yo-ho-ho, and a bottle of rum!' "**

Treasure Island by **R L Stevenson**

At the corner with Howe Street, look down the hill and you will see **St Stephen's Church (5)**

ST STEPHEN'S CHURCH dominates this central spine of the New Town. The church with its great tower was designed by the prolific architect William Playfair and finished around 1827 at a cost of almost £19,000. The tower boasts the longest pendulum in Europe. Playfair was also responsible for The Royal Scottish Academy and the The National Gallery of Scotland on Princes Street.

Walk up Queen Street Gardens West and turn right into Queen Street.

Number 52 Queen Street (6) was the home of **SIR JAMES YOUNG SIMPSON** (1811-70) after his marriage and his move from Stockbridge. A graduate of Edinburgh University, he became widely recognised as the Father of modern anaesthetics through his pioneering work with chloroform, although initially its use met with strong resistance. It was only after Queen Victoria asked to be anaesthetised during the birth of her 8th child, Prince Leopold, in 1853, that chloroform became more widely used. Simpson was Queen Victoria's personal physician for many years and was rewarded with a baronetcy in 1866 for his services. A portly gentleman with unkempt hair and whiskers, he achieved his ambition of leaving "footprints on the sands of time".

> **"I came to settle down a citizen of Edinburgh, and fight among you a hard and up-hill battle for life, for bread, and name, and fame, and the fact that I stand here before you this day so far testifies that in this arduous struggle- I have won".**
> Sir James Young Simpson
> on receiving the Freedom of the City of Edinburgh

Turn left into Castle Street.

NUMBER 39 CASTLE STREET (7) is where Sir Walter Scott lived periodically for about 25 years until 1826. Born in Edinburgh in 1771, he

39 Castle Street

was a polio victim in his early years and was educated at the Royal High School and Edinburgh University, where he studied law. His first novel, *Waverley*, was published anonymously in 1814 while Scott was visiting the Orkney Isles, and he returned to discover that it had become the most successful novel ever published in the English language. After his rise to prominence, Scott's main residence was the Gothic house of **Abbotsford** near Galashiels in the Borders, which he had acquired in 1812. Here he wrote many of his most famous works, including *Ivanhoe*, dictated during a period of illness, which sold 10,000 copies in two weeks. Abbotsford is open to the public and contains many of the curious items Scott collected, including **Napoleon's writing case** taken from his carriage at the battle of Waterloo, **a lock of Bonnie Prince Charlie's hair** and **Rob Roy's sword**. The magnificent house, however, merely added to the burden of debt that Scott laboured under after the collapse of the publishers Constable and Ballantyne, in which he had a large stake. It was at this time that he sold 39 Castle Street to ease his financial crisis. But Scott's was determination to pay off his debts of £130,000 by sheer hard work ruined his health. He died at Abbotsford in 1832, having had his bed moved to the dining room because its windows commanded the best view of the River Tweed. He spoke his last words to John Gibson Lockhart, his son-in-law:

> **"I may have but a minute to speak to you. My dear, be a good man - be virtuous - be religious - and be a good man. Nothing else will give you any comfort when you come to lie here."**

Continue up to George Street and turn right. Walk along to Charlotte Square.

In the centre of the Square is Sir John Steell's statue of **PRINCE ALBERT on horseback (8)**. It is well documented that Queen Victoria and Prince Albert enjoyed a devoted relationship, and also that Albert had a great deal of difficulty in finding acceptance with the British people. He did eventually develop his own role as a champion of the people after his successful Empire Exhibition in The Crystal Palace, but public displays of affection such as the statue in Charlotte Square were still a source of pleasure for the Queen. This statue earned John Steell a knighthood. He also designed many other statues in Edinburgh including the impressive **Duke of Wellington**, again on horseback, at the east end of Princes Street, and **Sir Walter Scott and his dog Maida** at the Scott Monument.

On the far side of the square is **WEST REGISTER HOUSE (9)** which was originally St George's Church. It is now used as a store for government documents, although there is a permanent display of historic Scottish documents open to the public. This modern use for the building, and the bank at the other end, means that Craig's original plan for magnificent churches facing each other down George Street will never be fulfilled. The exhibitions at West Register House are open from 10am-4pm, entry free.

To the left, at **16 SOUTH CHARLOTTE STREET (10)**, **ALEXANDER GRAHAM BELL** was born on March 3rd 1847. His early education at the Royal High School was continued in America, where he invented the telephone whilst working as a professor at the University of Boston. Bell also invented and patented the hydrofoil, which he unsuccessfully tried to sell to both the British and American Navies during the First World War. His invention did, however, set a new world water speed record of 70 mph in 1919, which was to stand for ten years. As a child, he invented the name **"H. A. Largelamb"**, an anagram of A. Graham Bell, and as an old man he used this name to start a secret career as a writer on science and technology for 'The National Geographic' magazine, but the secret soon leaked and his new career was over.

> Address to a graduation class at the age of 70:
> **"What a glorious thing it is to be young and have a future before you; it is also a glorious thing to be old and look back upon the progress of the world during one's own lifetime. I myself, am not so very old yet, but I can remember the days when there were no telephones."**
> Alexander Graham Bell

At the far side of the square, Douglas Haig, better known as **EARL HAIG**, was born in 1861 at **No. 24 Hope Street (11).** An army man through and through, he fought in the Boer war in South Africa, then served in Egypt and India before taking over from Sir John French as Commander of the British Forces on the Western Front during the First World War. Today, Haig remains one of the most controversial figures of the era, who believed that his military decisions were divinely inspired, and whose strategy cost the lives of thousands of British soldiers in a pointless war of attrition.

THE GENERAL (1)

"Good-morning, good morning!" the General said
When we met him last week on our way to the line.
Now the soldiers he smiled at are most of 'em dead,
And we're cursing the staff for incompetent swine.
"He's a cheery old card," grunted Harry to Jack
As they slogged up to Arras with rifle and pack.

But he did for them both by his plan of attack.

NO. 7 CHARLOTTE SQUARE (12) is a typical Georgian House, fully restored by the National Trust for Scotland and open to the public. It stands in what is arguably the finest row of Georgian houses ever built. Numbers 1-11 Charlotte Square were designed around 1791 by Robert Adam who brought the end houses out and created a masterpiece of proportion in the classical style. Adam was also successful in his more mundane architectural work, designing public buildings, and shades of his Charlotte Square design can be seen in Register House at the east end of Princes Street. No.5 Charlotte Square is the headquarters of the National Trust, No.6 is the Secretary of State for Scotland's official residence, and No.7 is well worth visiting for a taste of Georgian Scotland. (Summer opening times: Mon-Sat 10am-5pm; Sun 2-5pm; entry £1.60)

---

(1) The General by **Selgfrled Sassoon**, Denmark Hill Hospital, 1917.

4

Calton Hill and Princes Street

The Athens of the North
New Register House
Waverley Market
The Scott Monument
Jenners
The National Gallery & R.S.A.
Princes Street Gardens

RECOMMENDED CAFES & BARS
The Coffeeshop (above Top Shop), 30 Princes Street
Penguin Cafe, 26 Frederick Street
Next Cafe, 119 Princes Street
The Cornerstone Cafe, St John's Church

Starting Point: **CALTON HILL (1).**

CALTON HILL inspired the popular description of Edinburgh as 'The Athens of the North'. It is a curious collection of useful buildings, monuments and follies built on a hard volcanic plug of rock which, like the Castle Rock and Arthur's Seat, was resistant to glacial erosion. The original volcanic activity took place around 350 million years ago during the Carboniferous Period, and the Quaternary glaciation has left the classic crag and tail landscape with a gentle east facing slope which provides access. This has given Calton Hill a dominant position at the east end of Princes Street and excellent views all around the city.

THE NATIONAL MONUMENT, by William Playfair, is a copy of the Parthenon which was built as a monument to the men who fell in the Napoleonic Wars. The foundation stone was laid in 1822, but work was suspended in 1830 when the money ran out. Stark, massive, and uncompromising, the twelve columns suggest the ruin of some ancient civilisation.

THE OLD OBSERVATORY was the work of James Craig, architect of the central New Town. Designed in 1776 in the style of a gothic fortress, it is a radical departure from his earlier classical work.

The much larger **NEW OBSERVATORY** is cruciform in shape, with prominent Doric columns and the characteristic green dome to house the telescopes. This astromonical temple was designed by Playfair in 1818. It was superceded by the observatory at Blackford Hill to the south of the city (see Hermitage of Braid walk).

The telescope shaped **NELSON MONUMENT** was completed in 1819 and commemorates Admiral Lord Nelson, who was killed at the battle of Trafalgar in 1805. On top of this unusual structure is a time ball which, before the introduction of the 1 o'clock gun at Edinburgh Castle, was lifted and dropped to show mariners the precise time of day. The time ball still works, but is no longer in use. Also of note is the stone flagship above the door.

THE DUGALD STEWART MEMORIAL was built to honour Edinburgh University's Professor of Moral Philosophy in the late 18th century. This elaborate structure is a copy of another Greek monument, that of Lysicrates, as is the Burns memorial just down the hill in Regent Road.

Also of note are the Doric monument to **JOHN PLAYFAIR**, mathematician and president of the Astronomical Institution, and the Portuguese cannon which replaced the Russian gun that originally stood here.

Walk down the steps to the bottom of the hill and cross the road to where the imposing St Andrew's House stands (a government building and part of the Scottish Office). Turn right and continue on to the **Old Calton Burial Ground (2).**

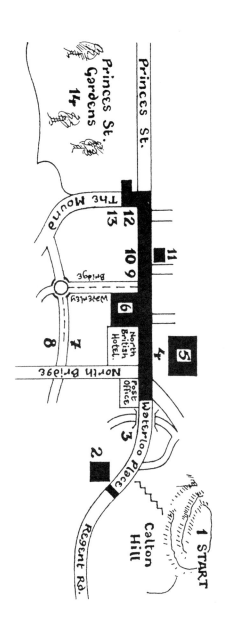

Princes St.

Princes St.
Gardens
14

The Mound

12
13

10 9

11

Bridge

Waverley

6

North
British
Hotel.

8

7

5

4

North Bridge

Post
Office

3

Waterloo Place

2

Regent Rd.

Calton
Hill

1 START

27

CALTON CEMETERY has the first statue of Abraham Lincoln to be erected outside the United States of America, commissioned as part of the memorial to the Scottish Americans who died during the American Civil War. To the left of the statue is the tomb of the philosopher David Hume (see New Town walk), and his far from modest memorial is a Robert Adam design dating from 1777. Another memorial which is difficult to miss is the enormous obelisk which dominates the cemetery. This is the Martyrs' Monument of 1844 which is there to remind us of the political martyrs of 1793 whose quest for political reform led to their conviction for sedition and subsequent transportation.

> *Continue down Waterloo Place and across* **Regent Bridge (3)***, another Napoleonic War memorial. Stop at the Post Office and across the road is the Wellington statue and Register House beyond.*

THE DUKE OF WELLINGTON on his horse **COPENHAGEN (4)** is a statue by Sir John Steell which dates from 1852. It is technically interesting in its use of the horse's tail as a balancing point with which to achieve the dramatic prancing effect. **REGISTER HOUSE (5)** is another Robert Adam design and one of his most highly regarded works. It was built with money confiscated from the Jacobites after their defeat at Culloden and completed in 1827, over 50 years after the work was started. It is now a store for official documents, which include Scotland's copy of the 1707 Treaty of Union with England. (Open 9am-4.30pm, admission free)

New Register House (entrance on West Register Street) can advise on how best to trace Scottish ancestry. Birth, death and marriage registers can be examined on request.

> *Continue along Princes Street, and on the left is Waverley Market (6).*

WAVERLEY MARKET is the home of the Tourist Information Centre and some excellent small shops. It is relatively new and sells all sorts of books, clothing, knitwear and food in a post-modernist 'designer' setting. A detour down Waverley Bridge and left into Market Street will take you to the **FRUITMARKET GALLERY (7)** and the **CITY ART CENTRE (8)** opposite. These galleries show avant-garde contemporary work in a

Dugald Stewart Memorial

29

variety of media, including installations, video, painting and sculpture.

Back at Princes Street, continue past Waverley Bridge and on the left is the statue of **David Livingstone (9).**

DR. DAVID LIVINGSTONE was one of the most famous of the 19th century explorers who sought to open up the 'Dark Interior' of Africa. He set out on an expedition to find the source of the Nile in 1866 and was not heard of for several years until he was found by the American journalist and adventurer **H. M. Stanley** in 1871, who found a "pale and wearied" man in grey tweed trousers and greeted him with the immortal words **"Dr Livingstone, I presume?"** Born in 1813, it was his missionary work which originally took him to Africa and led to his crossing of the Kalahari Desert and subsequent discovery of Victoria Falls via the Zambezi River. Despite his frequent expeditions, Livingstone found time to marry, and he wrote of his wife Mary that she was "not romantic, but a matter-of-fact lady, a little, thick, black-haired girl, sturdy and all I want". In 1857 he was made an honourary Burgess, or freeman, of Edinburgh, and it was after this that his trip to find the sources of the Nile ran into trouble. Stanley tried to persuade him to return home, but with his wife already dead, Africa had become his home. The last entry in his journal was: "tried to ride, but was forced to lie down, and they carried me back to the village exhausted". He died soon afterwards in 1873, and was interred in Westminster Abbey.

Next to the statue is **the Scott Monument (10).**

THE SCOTT MONUMENT, or Gothic Rocket, was designed by George Miekle Kemp and completed in 1844 at a cost of £15,650. Dedicated to Sir Walter Scott, the marble statue of the great novelist and his dog Maida, by Sir John Steell, is surrounded by historical figures and characters from his own novels carved onto the monument itself. The monument is open to the public and it is possible to climb to the top, 200 feet above Princes Street. (Summer 9am-6pm; winter 9am-3pm; entry 50p)

Across the road is **JENNERS (11),** Edinburgh's most famous department store.

Continue along Princes Street to the classical **R.S.A. building (12)** *and* **The National Gallery (13).**

THE ROYAL SCOTTISH ACADEMY is another neo-Classical William Playfair design, completed in 1826. The statue above the entrance is of Queen Victoria, and is by one of her favourites, Sir John Steell (also responsible for Prince Albert in Charlotte Sq). The Academy holds an annual exhibition of its member's work. (Open Mon-Sat 10am-9pm; Sun 2-5pm; entry £1.20)

THE NATIONAL GALLERY OF SCOTLAND houses a very fine collection of paintings. The Old Masters are represented here as well as the Impressionists and Scottish artists, all the pictures dating from between 1400 and 1900. There are Titians, Rembrandts, Reubens, Gainsboroughs, Raphaels and Poussins, as well as works by Degas, and Delacroix. Particularly worthy of note are **Monet's** *Poplars on the Epte*, and the unique **Vaughan Bequest** of Turner watercolours which are only shown on request (Mon-Fri 10-12.30 & 2-4.30pm). The building was designed, once again, by William Playfair, and the collection is rightly described as one of the best in Europe. (Open Mon-Sat 10am-5pm; 2-5pm Sun; entry free)

Cross at the traffic lights next to the R.S.A. and walk down the steps into **Princes Street Gardens (14)**, *which is the end of this walk.*

On the right is the **FLORAL CLOCK**, built in 1903, which is the oldest in the world. **PRINCES STREET GARDENS** are where the Nor' Loch used to be, the almost stagnant lake that in more violent times proved an excellent deterrent against aggressors. It was drained in the late 1700's as the New Town was being built, and Princes Street was a residential road at the time. The residents fought hard to make sure that the site was not built upon, and an Act of Parliament passed in 1827 ensured that the new gardens would remain in perpetuity. As Princes Street developed into a commercial centre the gardens also flourished, and are now a much prized public amenity.

A stroll through the gardens will reveal the Ross Bandstand, a statue of **Thomas Guthrie** (who started the 'Ragged Schools' and campaigned against liberal drink laws), a statue of **Sir James Young Simpson** (who pioneered modern anaesthetics), and various war memorials. Among the most interesting of these are the statue of the mounted trooper wearing a bearskin, which commemorates the Scots Greys campaigns during the Boer War (1899-1902) and the World Wars, the memorial to the Scots who fought in 1914-18, and the boulder which is a memorial to the Norwegian Brigade and other army units trained in Scotland.

**"Here we found hospitality, friendship and
hope during dark years of exile"**
Norwegian Memorial

**"If it be life that waits,
I shall live forever unconquered,
If it be death I shall die at last,
Strong in my pride and free."**
The Call
First World War Memorial

At the far end, past the Simpson statue is **St. John's Episcopal Church**, next to Lothian Road. The interior of this William Burn building is its best feature, and it is here that **Sir Henry Raeburn**, the renowned Scottish portrait painter, is buried.

5

Grassmarket to Greyfriars

Ancient Market & Execution Site
Victoria Street Shops
The National Library
The Royal Museum of Scotland
Greyfriars Bobby
Greyfriars Churchyard
George Heriot's School

Starting Point: *THE GRASSMARKET* (1)
CITY CENTRE 3/4 MILE

RECOMMENDED CAFES & BARS
Helios Fountain, 7 Grassmarket
Byzantium, 9a Victoria Street

This part of Edinburgh has seen both peaceful and bloody times. In 1477 James III designated **the Grassmarket** as a suitable site for markets to be held. For about 200 years commerce continued without hindrance, and the area was a regular meeting place for farmers and traders. But around 1660, the public execution site was moved from Castle Hill to the much larger Grassmarket site because of the increasing popularity of public hangings. **Half-Hangit Maggie** (see Duddingston walk) cheated the gallows here, and many **Covenanters** died here for their faith. In 1736 the Grassmarket witnessed the famous **Porteous Riot.** Incensed at the hanging of a smuggler, Andrew Wilson, the crowd became increasingly vocal and decided to take action. The mob advanced and the captain of the guard ordered his men to fire into the crowd. Six died. Captain John Porteous was tried and condemned to death for his actions, but later received a Royal Pardon. This was the last straw, and the mob re-formed, dragged Captain Porteous from the Tolbooth and hanged him in the Grassmarket. He is buried in Greyfriars Churchyard. The ringleaders were never caught.

"On the day when the unhappy Porteous was expected to suffer the sentence of the law, the place of execution, extensive as it is, was crowded almost to suffocation. There was not a window in all the lofty tenements around it...that was not absolutely filled with spectators. The uncommon height and unique appearance of these houses, some of which were formerly the property of the Knights Templar and the Knights of St John and still exhibit on their fronts and gables the iron cross of these orders, gave additional effect to a scene in itself so striking. The area of the Grassmarket resembled a huge dark lake or sea of human heads, in the centre of which arose the fatal tree, tall, black, and ominous, from which dangled the deadly halter."

The Heart of Midlothian by **Sir Walter Scott**

No executions have taken place here since 1784, but the site is marked by rose coloured stones in the form of a Cross of St Andrew by the railings, where there is also a roll of honour and a brief explanation of the events of the time.

Both Robert Burns and William Wordsworth stayed in the White Hart Inn when they visited the city, and the pub is still open for business.

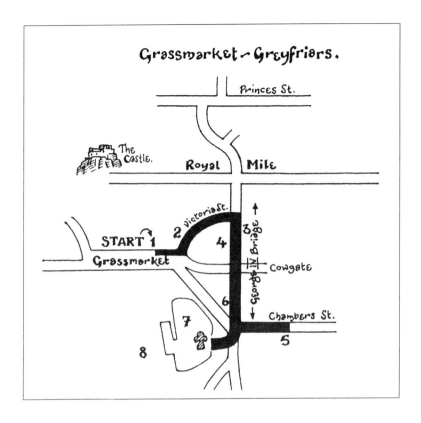

Grassmarket ~ Greyfriars.

Princes St.

The Castle.

Royal Mile

Victoria St.

START 1

2

4

3 George IV Bridge

Cowgate

Grassmarket

6

7

Chambers St.

8

5

Walk up **Victoria Street (2)**

VICTORIA STREET is a charming street, with a wide range of unusual gift shops, coffee shops and craft and antique shops. Byzantium has a good selection of small specialist shops, and there are some first-class bars and restaurants.

At the top of Victoria Street turn right onto George IV Bridge.

GEORGE IV BRIDGE was designed by Thomas Hamilton and opened in 1836 in response to the City Improvement Act which recognised the need for better communications to the south. Its completion meant that traffic was not forced to go down the steep hills to the Cowgate.

On George IV Bridge, **the two libraries (3)** *and* **(4)** *can be seen. Across the road is the National Library.*

THE NATIONAL LIBRARY OF SCOTLAND stands opposite the Central Library. There has been a library here since the 17th century, although the present building was designed by Reginald Failie in the mid 1930's. Because of the onset of the Second World War, it took until 1955 to complete the building, but the exterior strongly reflects the architecture of the 1930's. A copy of every publication must be sent here, and its 4.5 million books make it one of the four largest libraries in Britain.

THE CENTRAL LIBRARY on the right, with the inscription "Let There Be Light", was built in 1890 using funds donated by Andrew Carnegie. It's a deceptive building because although its entrance is on George IV Bridge, its lower levels are on the Cowgate several floors below. The Edinburgh Room is devoted to the history and culture of the city, and contains many fascinating books, maps and documents. If in doubt, try here.

Cross the road and continue along to Chambers Street, turn left and walk along to the **Royal Museum of Scotland (5)** *on the other side of the road.*

Facing the museum is a statue of **WILLIAM CHAMBERS**, the publisher and Lord Provost of Edinburgh after whom this street is named. Chambers was born in 1800, and on arrival in Edinburgh became an apprentice bookseller. After his 5 year training, he found it difficult to find work and had no money to start his own business. He was lucky enough to find a London trader prepared to give him credit, and opened a shop shortly afterwards. From the small profit he made he bought a printing press, and published his first book: *The Songs of Robert Burns*. The 750 copies were printed and bound by Chambers himself and sold for a shilling. It was, of course, a success, and reaped a £9 profit. From this he went on to print posters: *To Let, Dog Lost, Fresh and Cheap*; and also published his brother

Robert's *The Traditions of Edinburgh*, which became another bestseller. Further success with the weekly *Chambers Journal* and *Chambers Information for the People* led to financial security. His most important public work was the restoration of St Giles Cathedral, on which he spent £30,000 of his own money, and the Chambers Aisle is a permanent memorial. The restorations he commissioned were finished in 1883, but Chambers died just a few days before the opening ceremony. The first service to be held was his funeral.

THE ROYAL MUSEUM OF SCOTLAND has large and wide ranging collections of animals, machinery and treasures, and is housed in yet another splendid Victorian building. But architecturally it is the Main Hall which is its crowning glory. Open 10am-5pm Mon-Sat; 2-5pm Sun; entry free.

> *Walk back up Chambers Street. Opposite is the statue of* **Greyfriars Bobby (6)** *with* **Greyfriars Churchyard (7)** *beyond.*

GREYFRIARS BOBBY is the world's most famous Skye Terrier. When he was only 2 years old, his master, John Gray (Old Jock), died. Such was Bobby's devotion to Old Jock, the local policeman, that despite the efforts of the church warden to keep the dog out of the churchyard, he always managed to find a way in so that he could be at his master's graveside. Soon his efforts made him famous throughout the city, and eventually the Lord Provost presented him with a dinner dish and a collar with a brass nameplate which exempted him from the dog licence for all time. The local tavern owner, a friend of Jock's, fed the dog every day, and Bobby died at the age of 16 on the 14th Jan 1872, 14 years after Old Jock. He is remembered as a remarkably dedicated dog, and his collar and dish are kept in the Huntly House Museum. The statue on George IV Bridge was renovated as a result of the renewed interest in the story after Disney made a film about the celebrated terrier.

GREYFRIARS CHURCH AND CHURCHYARD (7). The Kirk was built in 1620 and restored in 1938, and it stands on the site of a Franciscan Friary dating from the mid 15th century. The best route around the churchyard is to turn right at the entrance and walk around the perimeter.

The Churchyard.

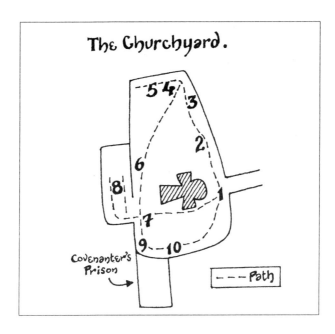

1 **Greyfriars Bobby**
2 **John Gray** - Bobby's owner.
3 **The Martyrs' Monument** - Commemorates the thousands of
   religious martyrs executed in Edinburgh.
4 **James Craig** - winner of the competition to design a New Town.
5 **Earl of Morton**- Regent to James VI, executed for his part in
   the political intrigues which surrounded Mary Queen of Scots.
6 **John Porteous** - Sparked off the Porteous Riot in the Grassmarket
   and paid with his life.
7 **Walter Scott**- Edinburgh solicitor and father of Sir Walter Scott.
8 **William Creech**- Published the works of Robert Burns and
   Adam Smith the economist, and became extremely rich in the process.
9 **The Adam Mausoleum**- William Adam, who designed the City
   Chambers, and was Robert Adam's father.
10 **Sir George MacKenzie**- Known as 'Bluidy MacKenzie',
   prosecutor of the Covenanters. In this mausoleum a boy spent 6 weeks
   after escaping from prison. Nobody looked here because the tomb is
   believed to be haunted.

George Heriot' s School can be seen from Greyfriars Churchyard. Heriot, known as *Jinglin' Geordie*, was the Royal Goldsmith and a money lender. After his death, his fortune was used to build this schoool for the education of fatherless boys, and it was completed in 1659. It was used by **Cromwell** as a military hospital before it was ever used as a school. During the school's summer holidays, some of the pupils organise tours (check at gate for details), which provide a rare opportunity to explore the school's history, as well as the strange optical illusion through the chapel keyhole.

New Town

Dean Village

St Giles

Stockbridge

Canongate

The General

Greyfriars

Cramond

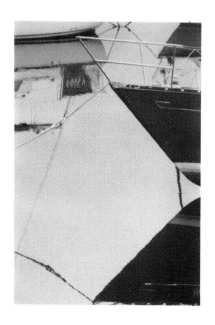

Cramond

Royal Mile

6
Stockbridge

The Water of Leith Walkway
The Colonies
Edinburgh Academy
James Clerk Maxwell
Stockbridge Market
Sir Henry Raeburn
Ann Street
St Bernards Mineral Well

Starting Point: ***THE T.S.B. BESIDE
STOCK BRIDGE (1).***
Bus: 28,29 from Hanover Street
34,35,80 from George Street

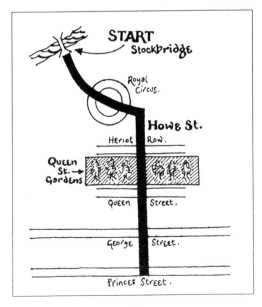

RECOMMENDED CAFES & BARS
The Bailie, St Stephen Street
Bib & Tucker, 2 Deanhaugh Street
Mortimer's Coffee Shop, Raeburn Place

STOCK BRIDGE. This bridge over the Water of Leith is only around 200 years old, but it has turned what used to be a quiet agricultural backwater into an extremely popular and affluent suburb which is now in the heart of the city. Since its creation, the bridge has undergone a series of improvements, the most recent at the turn of the century when it was widened to cope with the increasing volume of traffic. **The TSB building (2)** was built about 1840, but the interesting additions, the clocktower and balustrades, date from 1900.

At the TSB side of the bridge, walk down the steps onto **The Water of Leith walkway (3)**. *This section of the walkway is relatively new, but is not as picturesque as the later section between Stockbridge and Dean Village. At the end of this section turn right onto Glenogle Road and walk along to Reid Terrace. These neat rows of houses are* **'The Colonies' (4).**

THE COLONIES, originally called the Whins (the local word for gorse bushes), were built in 1861 by the Edinburgh Building Cooperative in response to the need for better quality housing for local workers. The terraces are named after the scheme's initiators, like Hugh Reid (journalist and M.P.) and James Colville (stonemason and the Co-operative's first manager). This development was in marked contrast to the philanthropic movement, which was also providing workers housing around this time (as can be seen in Dean Village). At the Water of Leith beside where The Colonies now stand, the young Robert Louis Stevenson spent much of his boyhood fishing in and playing beside the water. He was born about a mile away at 7 Howard Place, still a privately owned house.

Opposite Dunrobin Place (halfway along The Colonies), turn right into Gabriel's Road (up the steps) and right again into Saxe Coburg Street

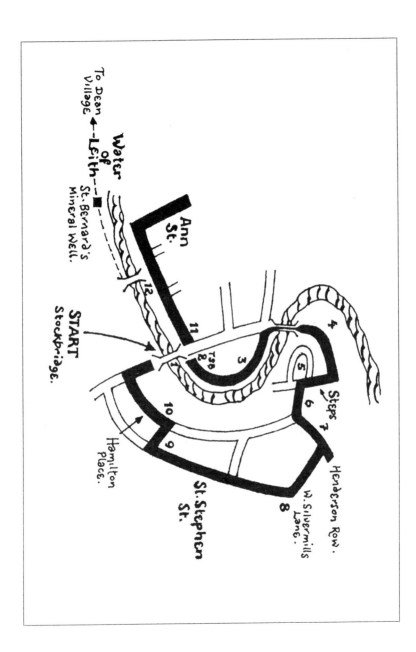

Saxe Coburg (5) is one of the prettiest Georgian Crescents in Edinburgh and reflects the New Town style. Before its existence, this was the site of a china ware factory, and examples of Stockbridge pottery can still be found in the Huntly House Museum on the Royal Mile.

Walk down Saxe Coburg Street and on the left is St Bernard's Church. **ST BERNARD'S CHURCH (6)** *is one of the oldest churches in the area. It was designed by James Milne who was also responsible for some of the architecture later on this walk, most notably Ann Street. The church was completed on 16th November 1823, and has a splendid facade with its Ionic pillars which support the pediment and the square clock tower.*

Continue to the end of Saxe Coburg Street and turn left into Henderson Row. On the left (about 50 yards on) is **Edinburgh Academy (7).**

EDINBURGH ACADEMY is one of an august body of fee paying schools in the city. The building itself was designed by William Burn and opened in 1824, and although it is not such an ornate building as George Heriots or some of the others, it is very much in the classical style of the New Town. It is said that the city Fathers objected to a private school being built to rival their own, and commissioned St Stephen's Church to block their view. One of the schools most famous pupils was **JAMES CLERK MAXWELL** (1831-1879) who ranks with Einstein and Newton in the scientific world, and was the author of *A Treatise on Electricity and Magnetism*, a seminal work. His family had an estate at Middlebie near Dumfries as well as a superb townhouse at **31 Heriot Row** and when he started at Edinburgh Academy the young James Clerk Maxwell had a strong Borders accent. This led to a difficult start at school, but his natural academic ability soon earned him a grudging respect from his peers. The adjacent building was the school for the deaf, but is more famous as the Marcia Blane School for Girls in the classic film *The Prime of Miss Jean Brodie*.

Cross the road and walk back towards Saxe Coburg Street. Turn left up West Silvermills Lane.

WEST SILVERMILLS LANE is a run down back street of Edinburgh in the late 20th Century, but it has a very long and occasionally prosperous history dating from before 1200. Its most recent history, and indeed its name, dates from when silver was discovered at Linlithgow (10 miles west of Edinburgh) in 1607. The refining of the silver ore was done here. Some traces of this way of life still remain to be seen as you walk here but when the ore ran out, the area was used for leather tanning. The lane acquired the rather insensitive nickname of Dumbie Street, because of the Deaf and Dumb Institute sited here.

At the top of West Silvermills Lane is **St Stephen's Church (8)**.

ST STEPHEN'S CHURCH dominates the area, and although strictly part of the New Town, it is difficult to ignore as you walk round Stockbridge. The church with its great tower was designed by the architect William Playfair and finished around 1827 at a cost of £19,000. Inside the church the two most notable features are the *Old Father Willis* organ of 1880, and the pendulum in the clock tower which is the longest in Europe. The site which was chosen for the church was rather cramped, so St Stephen's had to be built slightly askew, but it nonetheless dominates this central spine of the city.

Walk down St Stephen Street past Cinderella's discotheque on the right. On the left is the Dance and Drama School.

ST STEPHEN STREET. Next to the Dance and Drama School is the old St Stephen School, most notable for the unusual bible on top of the building. St Stephen Street has an interesting mix of shops, bars and restaurants, including some good second hand shops. There is also The Astrology Centre at 60 St Stephen Street. At the end of street (on the corner with N.W. Circus Place) is *The Bailie*, one of the best pubs in Stockbridge.

Continue by walking down St Stephen Place. The archway is the start of the old **Stockbridge market (9)**, *now replaced by housing. Walk through the site of the old market to* **No.5 Hamilton Place (10).**

NO.5, and the public toilet next to it used to be the local police and fire stations. For many years a barrow was kept here to ferry home the local drunks.

Walk back to Stock Bridge and turn right over the bridge, then left into Dean Terrace.

NO.1 DEAN TERRACE (11) was the home of Sir James Young Simpson before his marriage, when he moved to Queen Street (see New Town walk). In the 19th century his pioneering work with chloroform was highly controversial, but he is now universally recognised as the Father of modern anaesthetics. He was also Queen Victoria's personal physician for many years as well as the first Scottish medical practitioner to be knighted. His body is interred in Westminster Abbey.

Continuing along Dean Terrace, the bridge on the left is **St Bernards Bridge (12).** *Walk up Upper Dean Street, known as Mineral Street because of it's proximity to the mineral well, and on the right is Ann Street.*

ANN STREET is one of the most prestigious residential roads in Edinburgh. It is yet another superb example of Georgian architecture. This part of Stockbridge was conceived by Sir Henry Raeburn and designed by James Milne. Ann Street was named after Sir Henry's wife.

SIR HENRY RAEBURN lived in Stockbridge for most of his life and was responsible for much of the layout. He was the most famous portrait painter of his generation, and his talent was recognised at an early age by Sir Joshua Reynolds who advised him to go to Italy to study art. This he did for two years under the supervision of Pompeo Battoni (some of whose work hangs in the National Portrait Gallery on Queen Street). On his return to Edinburgh, his talent led to an unending number of commissions which lasted throughout his lifetime and brought him great wealth. His work rate was phenomenal, and some of his best work is on view in the Scottish National Portrait Gallery on Queen Street.

SIR JOHN WATSON GORDON lived at both No.17 and No.27 Ann St. He often met Sir Henry Raeburn at the mineral well and walked up to

Ann Street

town with him, discussing painting as they went. Sir John later became President of the Royal Scottish Academy.

DR. ROBERT CHAMBERS, the prolific author, was another famous resident of Ann Street. Robert, and his enterprising brother **William**, came from a well-to-do family, but their father's cotton manufacturing business failed when they were both young. They moved to Edinburgh to a life of poverty, where William became an apprentice bookseller, and Robert tried to pursue his academic interests. Their luck changed when William bought a small printing press and printed 750 copies of *The Songs of Robert Burns*, which quickly sold out. With the profits from this he published his brother Robert's *The Traditions of Edinburgh*, which was another best seller. Sir Walter Scott called on them with his congratulations, despite the fact that he had been preparing notes on the same subject for several years. William and Robert Chambers went on to publish the *Chambers Journal*, a weekly informative magazine which cost 1d at a time when *The Scotsman* cost 10d, and circulation soon rose to over 80,000 copies. Then *Chambers Information for the People* was published in 1834, and was even more successful. The brothers became pillars of Edinburgh society, and the publishing company they founded is still successful.

Walk back to **St Bernards Bridge** *and down the steps to the right to the Water of Leith Walkway. Walk along the path until you reach St Bernard's Mineral Well.*

The foundation stone of **ST BERNARD'S MINERAL WELL** was laid on the 15th September 1760, and the quality of water was said to rival any in Britain. The structure that can be seen today is a slightly later version, designed to reflect a temple at Tivoli in Italy and finished appropriately with a statue of **Hygeia**, the Greek Goddess of health. The water was available to all the citizens of Edinburgh, although those who could afford to pay were charged a penny a day. The bathing of sores was not permitted. It was to prove a profitable business at that time, because the medicinal properties of the water were widely believed to be life enhancing. The well is named after **St Bernard of Clairvaux**, of whom Luther said "If ever there lived on Earth a God fearing and Holy monk, it was St Bernard." He came to Scotland to try and raise support for the 2nd Crusade but his audience at Court proved less than fruitful, and he retired, exhausted and ill from travelling, to a cave near the present well. It is said that the local water revived him and restored him to full health and he continued on his way.

At this point there are three options available:

1) Walk back to the starting point at Stock Bridge.

2) Continue along the path past the small and much less imposing St. George's Well as far as Thomas Telford's towering Dean Bridge (details in Dean Village section)

3) Continue on to Dean Village and the next walk.

7
Dean Village

Thomas Telford's Dean Bridge
The Mills of Dean
The Baxters
Well Court
The Granary
Scottish National Gallery of Modern Art
Dean Cemetery

Starting Point: *KIRKBRAE HOUSE* (1)
at the top of Dean Bridge on the corner with Bell's Brae.
CITY CENTRE 1/2 MILE

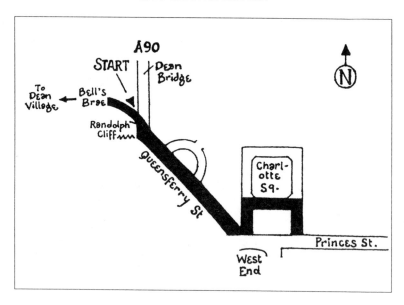

Dean Bridge provides a magnificent overview of the village, and at the far side of the bridge is **Holy Trinity Church (2)** which dominates the valley. Built in 1838 the congregation fell to just a handful during the war, and the church was sold during the 1950's. The building is currently being renovated after years of neglect.

At the top of the hill is **Kirkbrae House**. Evidence of the Baxters, or bakers, starts here, and at one time they had eleven watermills and two granaries operating in the valley. This was a perfect site for milling flour and baking which had the river as a source of power and was between the farms to the west and the customers in the city. This is one of the oldest parts of Edinburgh, dating from the time of **King David I** in the 12th century. The economic strength that the Baxters developed through their control of the city's bread supplies soon made them a powerful local Guild. At Kirkbrae House two of their symbols, the wheatsheafs and the ripening sun, can be seen, as well as the quotation from Genesis: "In the sweat of thy face shalt thou eat bread". Kirkbrae House was the Baxters House of Call, or Inn (now Cabbies Antiques).

Walk down Bell's Brae. This was the main road from the north and west into the city before Dean Bridge was built. At the bottom of the hill on the left is the **Baxters' Tolbooth (3)**.

THE BAXTERS' TOLBOOTH was the baker's headquarters. Here you will see the carved inscription "God's providence is our Inheritence", as well as "God bless the Baxters' of Edinburgh who built this house 1675". The other sign is the crossed peels or bakers' shovels (used to remove hot bread from the ovens) and three cakes and a pie, all symbols of their trade.

Next to the bridge is **BELL'S BRAE HOUSE (4)**, which is an excellent example of a 17th century house. It was restored this century by Sir Basil Spence for the Polish born artist Aleksander Zyw.

Walk along Miller Row until you get to the three round stones, then continue on to the bridge.

The three stones (5) on the left are grindstones, and are all that remains of Lindsay's Mill. On the right, the new office building is on the site of **'Jericho' (6)**, the city granary from 1619 which burnt down spectacularly in 1956. On the right under Dean Bridge is the castellated structure which is now the premises of **Oxylitre Ltd (7)**, and dates from 1912. Its original use was as a raquets or squash court, and it must have been one of the world's most ornate sports facilities.

DEAN BRIDGE (8) towers massively above the Water of Leith and stands in contrast to the small river it spans. Opened in 1832 and designed by Thomas Telford, it allowed much better communications with the land to the north of Edinburgh. Telford's right hand man on the project, John Gibb, was something of a character. He built a platform to inspect the work in progress and took particular pleasure in shouting at anyone whose work wasn't up to standard. If they dared to show dissent he would descend to argue the case, with his fists if necessary. This may be the reason the work was finished ahead of time, but the new bridge wasn't immediately opened to the general public as Gibb decided to charge a penny for access to the bridge until the official handing over ceremony. Because of the height of the bridge and the nature of the drop, it quickly became an alternative to Salisbury Crags for those with suicidal tendencies and a well developed sense of the dramatic.

Walk back to the start of Miller Row and cross the bridge. The first building on the right is **West Mill (9)**.

WEST MILL underwent its conversion in 1973. Originally built in 1805, the new apartments incorporate the old mill's features to good overall effect. The round windows once ventilated the grain that was being stored prior to milling, and it is a measure of the strength of the original building that it is still in use today.

Walk on, turn left into Damside and left again into **Well Court (10)**.

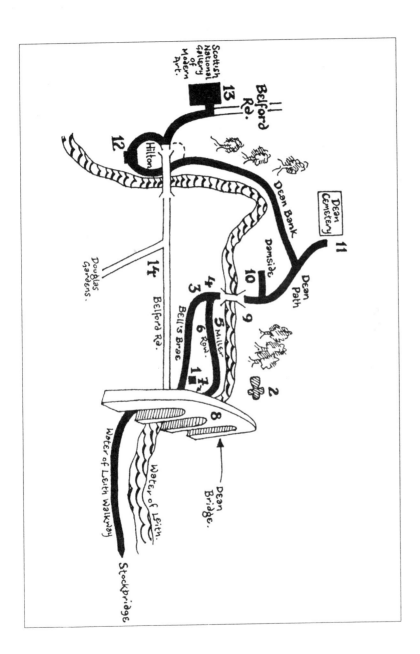

Scottish National Gallery of Modern Art.

13

Belford Rd.

12

Hilton

Dean Bank

Dean Cemetery

11

Damside.

Dean Path

Douglas Gardens.

14

Belford Rd.

10

9

4
3

Bell's Brae

5 Miller

6 Row

1

7

2

8

Dean Bridge.

Water of Leith Walkway

Water of Leith.

Stockbridge

IN MEMORY OF-
LIEUT JOHN IRV-
ING H M SHIP
TERROR BORN
1815 DIED 1848-9

HER MAJESTY'S SHIPS
EREBUS AND TERROR
LEFT ENGLAND IN MAY
1845 UNDER COMMAND
OF SIR JOHN FRANKLIN
KCB TO EXPLORE A
NORTH WEST PASSAGE
TO THE PACIFIC
AFTER WINTERING 1845-
6 AT BEECHEY ISL AND
THEY SAILED SOUTH
DOWN FRANKLIN'S
STRAIT AND ENTERED
THE NW PASSAGE HAV-
ING BEEN THERE BESET
WITH ICE FOR TWO
YEARS SIR J FRANKLIN 8
OTHER OFFICERS AND 15
SEAMEN HAVING DIED
THE SURVIVORS 105 IN
NUMBER LIEUT IRVING
BEING ONE LANDED ON
KING WILLIAMS LAND
AND ATTEMPTED TO
MARCH TO CANADA
BUT ALL DIED FROM
COLD AND WANT OF
FOOD IN 1879 LIEUT SCH-
WATKA OF THE AMERI-
CAN SEARCHING EXPE-
DITION DISCOVERED
LIEUT IRVINGS GRAVE.
THROUGH HIS KIND-
NESS THE REMAINS OF
THIS BRAVE AND
GOOD OFFICER WERE
BROUGHT AWAY AND
WERE DEPOSITED HERE
ON 7TH JANUARY 1881

It is interesting to compare the Colonies in Stockbridge with **WELL COURT** in Dean Village, both of which were an attempt to provide good housing for the workers. The architect here was Sidney Mitchell, but the motive force behind the work was **John Ritchie Finlay,** owner of The Scotsman newspaper. He was a philanthropist who took a great personal interest in the needs of working people. This is his most important work of this kind, and was in keeping with the mood of the 19th century which saw similar developments such as Cadbury's model village Bournville, and the Lever Brothers Port Sunlight near Liverpool. All these developments recognised the need for leisure time, hitherto a largely unrecognised concept, and provided facilities for social functions and meeting places.

Walk through the courtyard to the river. The unusual building opposite is the yellow, half-timbered Hawthorn Buildings which dates from around 1895. Return to Damside, then walk up the hill along Dean Path to the **DEAN BANK** *section of the Water of Leith walkway, or take a short detour via* **Dean Cemetery (11)** *at the top of the hill.*

Dean Cemetery is both attractive and ornate, with massive obelisks and a curious red granite pyramid. Many of Edinburgh's dignitaries and aristocrats are buried here, and there is an interesting memorial to a member of the Franklin expedition.

55   **Dean Cemetery**

Walking along the **DEAN BANK**, you can see the back of the Whytock and Reid Cabinet Works, the last of many local industries which also included a distillery and a wrought iron works. Most of the new developments have been housing and offices, not altogether surprising in view of the picturesque setting.

Walk under Belford Bridge, built in 1887, and round the corner on the right you will see the **Old Granary (12)**, *now part of the Hilton Hotel complex. The main entrance is on the far side.*

THE HILTON is built on the site of Bell's Mill which was devastated by a dust explosion in 1972. The granary (1807) survived and has been beautifully retored as a bar.

Continuing up the hill along Belford Road, the building on the left is the former John Watson's School, now the **Scottish National Gallery of Modern Art (13)**. David Hockney, Pablo Picasso, Barbara Hepworth, and Henry Moore are all represented here, as well as Samuel Peploe and other Scottish Colourists. There is also a gallery shop and an excellent cafe. (Open 10am-5pm; Sun 2pm-5pm; entry free.)

The quickest route back to the starting point is back down Belford Road, past the Hilton and straight on. On the corner with Douglas Gardens is the former **Belford Church (14).** *This was also designed by Sidney Mitchell, the architect of Well Court, and is worth seeing if only for its outrageous gargoyles.*

8
Cramond

The River Almond Walkway and Mills
Roman Cramond
Cramond Tower
Cramond House
Cramond Kirk and Manse
The Old Village
The Causeway and Cramond Island

4 MILES WEST OF CITY CENTRE
Bus: 66 (To Cramond Brig Hotel for section 1)
18,40,41 (To Cramond Village for section 2)
All from Charlotte Square
Car: A90 Queensferry Road towards Forth Road Bridge

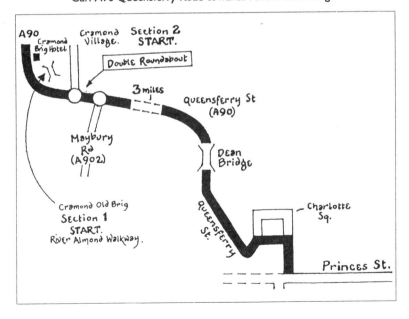

This walk is in three sections; the River Almond walkway, the village of Cramond itself and Cramond Island.

SECTION ONE - THE RIVER ALMOND WALKWAY

(40 Minutes Approx)

Starting point: The Cramond Brig Hotel on the A90 Queensferry Road. *Walk down through the car park to the Old Cramond Bridge.*

OLD CRAMOND BRIG dates from around 1500, but has been repaired and rebuilt on several occasions. Some of these dates can be seen carved on the parapets. Looking towards the new bridge, the ruins of **Jock Howieson's Cottage (2)** are visible beside the river on the left. It was near here that Jock Howieson went to the aid of a traveller who was being attacked by brigands, and drove them off. He took the injured man back to his cottage to let him recover. The traveller turned out to be King James V, who rewarded Jock with the substantial local estate of Braehead.

Cross over the bridge and turn left at the road, and then left again at Dowies Mill Lane, the start of the River Almond Walkway.

THE RIVER ALMOND, from the start of the walk right down to the village, was the main centre of milling and industrial activity in the area. It was here that the Industrial Revolution took hold for a brief time, and although iron was never made here, it was imported in reasonably large quantities to be used for the manufacture of nails and agricultural implements. The river offered the Industrialist a power source and, because the roads were either poor or non-existent, the sheltered harbour at Cramond as a way of moving raw materials in and finished products out to the markets. The scale of production was not enormous, and at its height between 1841 and 1851, the total workforce in the mills was about 95. Eventually, it was the river's physical limitations for expansion which led to the area's industrial demise.

The first buildings on the right are **DOWIES MILL COTTAGES (3)**. These date from around 1690 and overlook the weir which provided power for the original mill which stood just past the cottages. Formerly a grain mill, in 1750 it was converted for the production of spades.

The next mill was **PEGGY'S MILL (4)**, just around the corner from Dowies Mill. Very little remains of this former iron mill, which became a paper mill in 1815, but there are still the remains of foundations set in the path, as well as a water channel into the river. This mill lade which remains channelled the water to the 16 foot high water wheels and the forge-hammers which beat the bar-iron flat for processing.

On the far side of the river was **CRAIGIE MILL**, of which nothing visible remains.
From Peggy's Mill to **FAIR-A-FAR MILL (5)** is the longest walking section, and includes some beautiful scenery as well as a steep staircase over the intrusive cliff section. This is a ten minute walk.

FAIR-A-FAR weir is the next major landmark on the walk. An impressive 10 foot high construction, this cascade enabled the Fair-A-Far forge and furnace to continue working long after other mills on the Almond had changed over to steam power. Beside the weir, the ruin is that of the west forge which contained two furnaces, and on the south wall there are scrape marks showing the position of the wheel which worked the trip hammer. Another forge stood beside this one, and both these buildings appear in photographs taken in the 1920's. Fair-A-Far also had a tramway, or horse-drawn railway, down to the wharf at Cockle Mill, which transported raw materials and finished goods.

CADELL'S ROW of cottages (6) are next along the route and are named after the family who owned many of the local mills. Some of the family are buried in the churchyard and have iron gravestones made in the River Almond mills.

On the right is Schoolbrae which is the road up to Cramond Village itself, but before walking up the hill it is worth stopping at **Cockle Mill (7)** *on the left.*

59

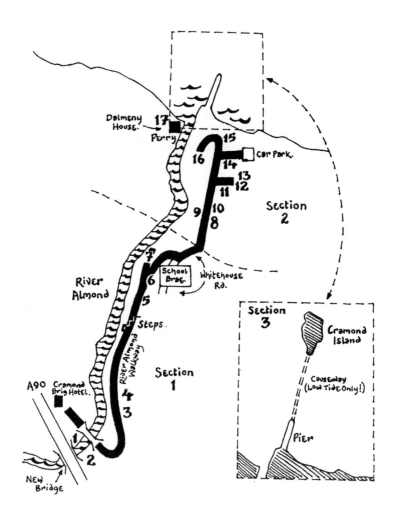

Dalmeny House.

17

Ferry

15

16

14

13

12

11

Car Park.

Section 2

10

9

8

7

6

School Brae.

Whitehouse Rd.

River Almond

5

Steps.

River Almond Walkway

A90

Cramond Brig Hotel.

4

3

Section 1

1

2

New Bridge

Section 3

Cramond Island

Causeway (Low Tide Only!)

Pier

60

COCKLE MILL is the final River Almond mill. Along with Cadell's Row, it is quickly being surrounded by new housing in this delightful setting. What remains (now as two houses) is the former mill office. The mill building itself, which stood next to the water, is long gone. The wharf was accessible only at high tide, and all the other mills had to bring their goods here for shipping. Up the hill is the old manager's house. From the making of nails, barrel hoops, anchors, pots and pans, spades, chains and agricultural implements, the Almond Mills saw bigger competitors emerge and could not expand to compete. Attempts at making paper, sawmilling and furniture production were only partially successful, and the area reverted once more to an agricultural way of life.

Walk up Schoolbrae past the mill manager's house on the right. Turn left at Whitehouse Road, and left again at Cramond Glebe Road.

SECTION TWO - CRAMOND VILLAGE

Walk down the hill along Cramond Glebe Road, and on the left (just past The Manse on the right) is the white painted **Old Schoolhouse (9).**

THE OLD SCHOOLHOUSE was built in 1778, at around the same time as the road. Upstairs was the schoolmaster's quarters where he and his family lived, and on the ground floor the pupils (between 70 and 80) were taught. The most famous teacher here was Mr. Ninian Paton, largely because he held the post for over 50 years. He is also remembered as a renowned smoker who not only rolled his own, but also grew his own tobacco plants in the garden to make sure of a regular supply. The school closed in 1875, and is now a private house.

Across the road is **Cramond Kirk and kirkyard (10)** *and the* **Manse next door (8).**

THE MANSE dates from the mid 17th century. Its most famous minister was the Reverend Robert Walker, minister from 1776 to 1784, known as the 'Skating Minister' and portrayed by Sir Henry Raeburn in action on

Duddingston Loch. (One of his predecessors, Adam de Gordon, incredibly managed to retain his position even after raping a local girl and killing a child with a spade.)

CRAMOND KIRK or Parish Church is on the site of the Roman fort, and there have been religious buildings here for many centuries. The mediaeval church fell into disrepair and a new one was built in 1656 which kept the 15th century tower at the west end. Since then sections have been added, like the castellations on the top of the tower in 1811. The most recent addition, the Session House was built in 1955. Inside the kirk, the most notable monument is a marble bust of Sir James Hope of Hopetoun House, who died in 1661.

THE KIRKYARD. The oldest stone is that of John Stalker (6th Feb. 1608), which can be found on the east wall. Many of the stones are typical of the 16th and 17th centuries, with their macabre memento mori - the skull and crossbones, hourglasses and angels. The Howison family, descendents of Jock Howison who saved the life of James V, are in the south east corner, as are the Cadells of the ironmills.

Continue down the hill. Through the gateway marked 'Kirk Cramond' on the right is the site of **the Roman fort (11)** *as well as* **Cramond House (12)** *and the* **Tower (13)** *(which is best viewed later on).*

THE ROMAN FORT was at the eastern side of The Antonine Wall, the most northerly Roman defence, and was a supply point chosen because of the natural harbour at Cramond. Emperor Antoninus Pius built the fort around 140 A.D. and although the Romans found it difficult to defend, they remained here until the 4th century. Full details of the fort, which was quite extensive, can be found at the site.

Past the Roman fort is **Cramond House (12).**

CRAMOND HOUSE was built in 1680, and in 1772 a new back and front were added to modernise its appearance and give it a classical grandeur. Queen Victoria really did sleep here on her way to and from Balmoral in

Cramond Tower

1860, because her mother, the Duchess of Kent, was in residence for the summer. The Queen, Prince Albert and the Duchess all attended Sunday service at Cramond Kirk. Today the house is the property of the Church and is used as the Beadle's Residence, and although at the moment it is not open to the public, there are plans to restore and open the top floor.

Walk back to the main road and continue down the hill. Turn right into the car park. On the right is the site of **the Roman bathhouse (14)** *which, sadly, has become overgrown and is almost completely hidden from view, largely due to a lack of excavation funds. Further on is the best view of* **Cramond Tower (13).**

CRAMOND TOWER is a 15th century tower originally owned by the Bishops of Dunkeld. It fell into disrepair but was recently retored by a local taxidermist and is now a very unusual and imposing private house.

Continuing down the hill, **CRAMOND INN (15)** on the right was a favourite haunt of Robert Louis Stevenson, and is still an excellent local hostelry.

Round the corner to the left is the harbour, Cramond Island and **The Maltings (16)**.

If you look up at the chimneys on the houses by the harbour, you will see that they are rather more numerous than might normally be expected. This is because inside the building each family had just a single room, so each room needed its own cooking facilities and therefore its own chimney. The Maltings has an exhibition run by *The Cramond Heritage Trust* on Saturday and Sunday afternoons in summer (open daily during the festival).

CRAMOND FERRY (foot passengers only, 9am-7pm in summer) takes visitors over to the Dalmeny Woods and the estate of the Earl of Rosebery, an excellent spot for picnicing. This is open to the general public, as is **DALMENY HOUSE** (open Sunday to Thursday 2- 5.30pm; phone 031-331 1888), although it's about a two mile walk there and back, so is perhaps best approached by car.

SECTION THREE - CRAMOND ISLAND

The 19 acre island is only accessible at low tide and the safe crossing times are posted on a notice board at the causeway. If you want to be sure of access, the times are available before you set off by phoning 0333 50666. Ownership of the island, currently the property of the Earl of Rosebery, was disputed by various groups of clergy for many centuries, and was mentioned in the Papal Bull of Pope Lucius as early as the 12th century. Cramond Island is worth visiting for its unusual Second World War fortifications and gun emplacements, but be careful of the treacherous tides. A walk across the causeway at low tide and round the uninhabited island is a rewarding, if somewhat eerie, experience.

The return to Old Cramond Brig is easiest by simply following the River Almond Walkway from the harbour.

9
Duddingston

The Innocent Railway
Duddingston Kirk and Manse
Bonnie Prince Charlie's Council of War
The Sheep Heid Inn
Mary Queen of Scots
Wildlife and Bird Sanctuary
Jacob's Ladder

2 MILES SOUTH EAST OF CITY CENTRE
Bus: 4A,42,43,44,45,46,47
Car: The Bridges, Clerk Street, Holyrood Park

SECTION I - THE INNOCENT RAILWAY

Starting point at *EAST PARKSIDE* in Holyrood Park Road
(near Commonwealth Pool).

*Walk into East Parkside (the Maltings) and turn first right and round
to the tunnel which is the start of the railway section.*

THE INNOCENT RAILWAY was unofficially christened 'Innocent' by
Dr. Robert Chambers because for the first few years of its existence the
carriages were horse drawn due to a deep suspicion of steam powered lo-
comotives. This is one of the earliest railways in Scotland, and a 500 yard
tunnel was a major engineering achievement in the early 19th century.
Edinburgh at this time was little more than a series of poorly intercon-
nected villages, so the impact of the railway in the 1820's and 1830's was
immense. Most importantly, it meant that the provision of coal for the city's
post industrial revolution energy needs was no longer a Herculean task.
The railway was originally intended simply as a commercial coal carrier and
there was no expectation of demand for a passenger service, but the idea
soon caught on. Only ten years after opening, around 300,000 passengers
a year were being carried on the line, all escaping the grime of the city for
the clean country air.

*Once through the tunnel, the rock formation up to the left is Samson's
Ribs.*

At **HANGMAN'S CRAG**, just on top of Samson's Ribs, one of Charles
II's hangmen met his end. The money he had inherited from his wealthy
Border's family did not last long, so he sought gainful employment.
Although suitable for very little, he did eventually find a job as the King's
executioner. Around this time, however, the King seemed eager to
execute religious and innocent men, and anyone willing to do his dirty work
became instantly unpopular. The conflict between the hangman's unpopu-

larity and his former high social position became more than he could bear when he tried to socialise with the gentlemen of the golf club and was ostracized. Unable to live with himself, his unpopularity and his terrible job he climbed Samson's Ribs and hurled himself to his death from the place now called Hangman's Crag.

Continue along the path. On the left after about half a mile is Bawsinch, rich with wildlife. On the right is Prestonfield golf course and hotel. Unfortunately this section of the walk is bounded by two high walls which spoil the view, although it's only a 15 minute walk to the end.

THE INNOCENT RAILWAY closed in the 1960's and very little use was made of it until the footpath was opened. At the far end of the railway section is a beautifully preserved cast iron bridge built in 1831 by the Shotts Iron Company.

Turn left at the end of the railway walk and continue up to the village.

SECTION 2 - DUDDINGSTON VILLAGE

Walk into the village by turning left at Old Church Lane. This site has been inhabited intermittently since the Bronze Age. The evidence for this was discovered in the loch and included various weapons, mostly spearheads, from around 700 BC. The modern development dates from around the 12th century when the monks of Kelso built the church, and the population started to grow around it.

HALF-HANGIT MAGGIE. In 1724 a Musselburgh fishwife, Maggie Dickson, was sentenced to death for the murder of her illegitimate child which was conceived and born while her husband was away working in Newcastle. She was taken to Edinburgh to be hanged. On the way back with the coffin , her friends stopped for a drink at Duddingston, but were astounded to see the body suddenly rise up and look about. Amazingly, she had survived the execution and was able to walk back to her home where she lived out the rest of her life with impunity and as a local celebrity.

Continue along Old Church Lane towards Arthur's Seat. On the left is the Manse, or **Minister's house (1).**

THE MANSE. About 200 years ago, the Manse was the focal point of the village, and the population was around 500. Through the years there have been many important visitors here, including **J.M.W. Turner** the landscape artist, and **Sir Walter Scott**, who is reputed to have written part of *Heart of Midlothian* in the Manse garden. It is certainly an inspiring setting. One of the most famous ministers here was the **Reverend John Thomson** (d. 1840) who moved from rural Ayrshire to take up a more exciting post near the capital. He was a very intelligent and sociable man who built up a fine parish, but is more famous for his landscape paintings, some of which can be seen in the National Gallery. With such public work it was very difficult for him to find time to paint, so he built a studio next to the loch and called it **"Edinburgh" (2)**, so that his housekeeper could tell visitors "he's not in, he's gone to Edinburgh". The small white studio still stands today.

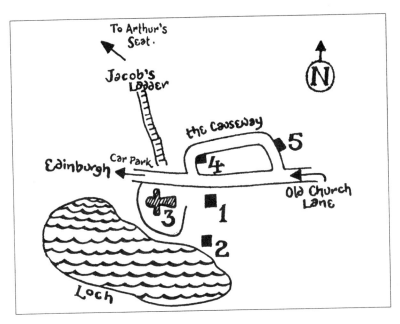

The next building on the left is **Duddingston Kirk (3),** *which has some original Norman architecture.*

THE KIRK. Before entering the churchyard it's worth looking at **the Watchtower** to the left of the gate. During the Burke and Hare bodysnatching era (before they made easier money by murdering and selling their victim's bodies for medical research), the church elders had to watch the churchyard for three weeks after a burial to make sure nothing was disturbed. Also at the gate (on the right) is the **'loupin'-on stane'**, a series of steps to help the ladies and elderly or overweight gentlemen on and off their horses, and the metal hoop and chain or **'joug's collar'.** This was used for parishoners' who misbehaved; adulterers, thieves &c, who were left chained on a Sunday to humiliate them in front of the whole village.

The kirk itself was built on land given to the Abbot of Kelso by King David I, and is one of the oldest in Scotland still in use. The original door is on the south side, now filled in, but the **Norman arch** with its chevrons and small carving of Christ can still be seen. The tower is not original but is certainly older than the 1631 north transept, not considered the kirk's best feature. One of the most interesting tombstones is near the present door and shows an unusual seascape.

Inside the church you can see the last remaining Norman feature, **the chancel arch** (also with chevrons), and the plaque on the wall remembering St. John William Keith who, at age 10, rescued his friend the Master of Saltoun but died in the attempt. It is said that an old man called at the Manse years later and asked for the key to the kirk where he sat and reflected on his long life. Before leaving he told the minister that he was the Master of Saltoun, returned to remember his friend and give thanks for his life.

From the churchyard there is a good view of the loch.

DUDDINGSTON LOCH

The loch, and Bawsinch beyond, is an official bird sanctuary (designated in 1925), and supports a great variety of wildlife, including **Greylag geese, mallards, partridges, heron and pochard** in winter. Long before this, though, in 1795, the Duddingston Curling Society was formed to formalise an already popular activity. The club attracted many men from the city: advocates, baronets, professors, and even **James Hogg** the poet and Ettrick Shepherd. Things went so well that W.H. Playfair, the prolific architect, was asked to design a clubhouse. But by 1850 many patrons were going to a new club at the West End, much closer to their city homes. **The skating minister of Cramond**, Rev. Robert Walker, was often to be found here, and was portrayed by Sir Henry Raeburn in action on Duddingston Loch.

Cross the Old Church Lane and walk down The Causeway, the village's other main street. Turn right and the first building is **The Sheep Heid Inn (4).**

THE SHEEP HEID INN is the oldest inn in Scotland and dates from 1360. It is still an excellent pub with a courtyard for fine days, and the building has retained its original character through the years. The name comes from the old Scottish delicacy of sheep's head which was eaten either boiled or baked. **James VI** was a frequent visitor at the inn and even presented a silver embossed ram's head to the owner. Another visitor was **Mary Queen of Scots**, who spent some time at nearby Craigmillar Castle (now ruined) and is said to have played indoor bowls at the Sheep Heid, an activity which still continues today.

Also on The Causeway, round the corner at the far end, is the restored **red tile house (5)** where **Bonnie Prince Charlie** held a council of war on 19th September 1745 before the battle of Prestonpans. The '45 rebellion was to prove a disaster, but Prestonpans was a great victory for the Scots over the English 'Auld Enemy', and Duddingston played its part. The battle is depicted in a painting at the Sheep Heid Inn.

SECTION THREE - THE RETURN WALK

*Walk back along The Causeway and turn right towards Arthur's Seat.
On the right, opposite the loch is Jacob's Ladder.*

1 The quickest return to **Holyrood Park Road**
is by following the main road.

2 By climbing **Jacob's Ladder** to the road
(Queen's Drive) and turning left you can return to
the starting point by walking along the top of
Samson's Ribs.

3 Alternatively, **Jacob's Ladder** is a good route
to the top of **Arthur's Seat**.

10
Hermitage of Braid

Superb Views of Edinburgh
Picturesque Park Walk
Hermitage House
Ice House
Observatory

Starting Point: **Braid Road**
near the corner with Hermitage Drive.

2 MILES SOUTH OF CITY
CENTRE
Bus: 5,11,15,16,17,23,41,51
Car: Lothian Road,
Morningside Road, Braid Road

**RECOMMENDED CAFES
& BARS**
None on the walk, although
Morningside Road has one of
Edinburgh's most unusual pubs,
The Canny Man

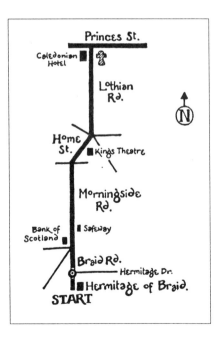

From the gatehouse, **Hermitage Lodge (1)** *(built 1880's), the path follows the Braid Burn. There is also a rough track down the other side of the water. Continue down the path to the first building on the left (public toilets). If you double back down the rough path and through the gap in the wall, the* **dovecot (2)** *is straight ahead up the steps into the wood.*

THE DOVECOT (DOOCOT). Although not the most beautiful of buildings, this was one of the largest dovecots in the Edinburgh area. Built on the site of an old castle, Fairlies of Braid (c.1340), the dovecot is late 17th century and provided the estate with a daily supply of fresh meat and eggs.

Back at the path, continue on to the visitor centre in Hermitage House

HERMITAGE HOUSE (3) was built in 1785 by a local builder, Charles Gordon, and because such a major construction was not designed by a famous architect it acquired the rather harsh description "Carpenter's Gothic". In 1938 the owner, John McDougall, gifted the house and grounds to the city, and there is now a permanent visitor display inside the house to explain the history and wildlife of the park.

Back at the path by the burn there are some steps up the bank to the right which lead to **the ice house (4)**.

THE ICE HOUSE. The import of ice into Scotland started at the beginning of this century, but before this the great houses all collected ice during the winter and stored it for use in summertime. It's construction is illustrated at the entrance.

The next section is through the wooded gorge. When you reach the large wooden bridge which crosses both the river and the path, walk under it, turn sharp left and up the hill. Continue until the path forks. The left fork goes round the corner to a steep grassy ascent to the top of **Blackford Hill (5)**, *but the right fork is a far more gentle climb.*

BLACKFORD HILL. At 538ft above sea level, Blackford Hill is hardly a

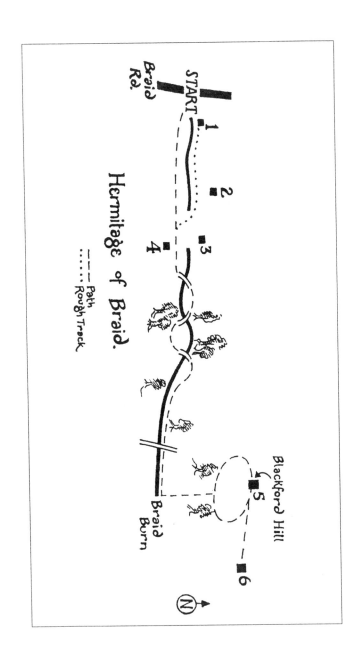

Hermitage of Braid.

Braid Rd.

START

Braid Burn

Blackford Hill

——— Path
······ Rough Track

N

mountain, but it does provide the most stunning views of the city. The hill is volcanic in origin, and like the Castle Rock and Calton Hill, was a vent of the main volcanic activity at Arthur's Seat. In 1987 the A.A. provided a viewing point which shows the location and distance of many important landmarks, and points out various mountains such as Ben Venue (2386 ft) at 53 miles and Ben Ledi (2882 ft) 49 miles away. As the anemometer, or wind speed machine, will testify, it can be quite windy near the top, but there are plenty of sheltered areas for picnicing. From the north side of Blackford Hill you can see Blackford pond below, a favourite local duck feeding spot.

Down the hill (to the east) is the **Royal Observatory (6)** *with its familiar light green domes.*

THE ROYAL OBSERVATORY. The visitor centre is open 7 days a week (Mon-Fri 10-4 : Sat/Sun 12-5 : adults £1). The permanent exhibitions and displays and the excellent selection of photos provide an insight into modern astronomy and space research.

The walk back down the hill to Hermitage of Braid is a gentle stroll returning you through the park to the starting point.

AN ALTERNATIVE ROUTE for those not wanting to walk through the park is to drive to the Observatory from where it's an easy walk to the top of Blackford Hill.

11
Holyrood Park and Arthur's Seat

Arthur's Seat
Salisbury Crags
St Anthony's Chapel
St Margaret's Loch

CITY CENTRE I MILE
Bus: 1,6,24
Car: Royal Mile

This park provides an excellent escape from the city whilst still being very close to the centre. Its history is closely connected with the kings of Scotland, although there are numerous theories about the origin of the name Arthur's Seat, the park's and Edinburgh's highest point. There was a **King Arthur** in central Scotland around 500 A.D., so it could be connected with him, or perhaps it's from the Gaelic *Ard-na-Saigheid* - the height of an arrow's flight. Nobody really knows. What is known is that the park was the property of Holyrood Abbey, and covers about 650 acres.

In 1540, the park became **James V's Royal Game Reserve** and was enclosed and barred to the general public. Later, during the city's great plague, Holyrood Park became an open air hospital although many died either of disease or exposure and were buried within the confines of the park partly in an attempt to contain the plague, and partly because there wasn't anywhere else to bury the dead. During the 1820's the Salisbury Crags were quarried, and it was ten years before this opportunistic work was stopped. About the same time **The Radical Road** was built around Salisbury Crags. This work was instigated by **Sir Walter Scott** to combat the frustration felt by local unemployed craftsmen during an economic slump, and it is after their radical views that the road is named. The main driveway, Queen's Drive, was named in honour of Queen Victoria. More recently in the park's history, some of the location shots for the James Bond film *From Russia With Love* were taken at Arthur's Seat.

Geologically, **Arthur's Seat** is the central core, or plug, of a long extinct volcano, and is made of a hard basaltic rock. The softer surrounding rock was swept away by the Ice Age glaciation, and the result is a highly dramatic series of formations. All this happened over 200 million years ago, and since then the rock has changed shape due to the Earth's movement and extensive erosion. Natural history details can be found at the entrance to the park (near the Palace gates) in the **Scottish Wildlife Trust's Visitor Centre.**

Starting Point: BESIDE THE PALACE OF
HOLYROODHOUSE.

Walk into the park and turn left. Cross the road and continue along Queen's Drive. The first point of interest is **St.Margaret's Well (1).**

ST MARGARET'S WELL was originally at Restalrig, but was moved in 1862 because of developments on the North British Railway. It is named after the wife of King Malcolm III, and dates from the 15th century.

Continue along to **St Margaret's Loch (2)**

ST. MARGARET'S LOCH was artificially created, much to the delight of the swans, ducks and other wildlife which have made it their home. It perfectly enhances the rather forlorn looking **ST ANTHONY'S CHAPEL (3)** and the hermitage beside it which date from about 1430. Little is known about these ruins, except that they are probably named after **St Anthony the Eremite** and have been uninhabited for the last few hundred years, but the religious order who lived here must have been extremely hardy to survive the winters.

"In the King's Park, on the declivity of Arthur's Seat, was a beautiful Chapel of Gothic architecture, consecrated to St Anthony; and there was a Hermitage adjoining to it, wherein a succession of anchorets, who have rested this weary age, lived remote from all the pleasures of a guilty world."

Dr Chalmers in *Caledonia*

The best way to the top is simply to keep going up the 'Lion's Haunches' towards 'The Lion's Head'. At the top of **Arthur's Seat** *is a viewpoint which shows the various landmarks as far as the Highlands. But if you don't want to walk to the top, there are plenty of other routes to explore, like the Radical Road, in this historic park.*

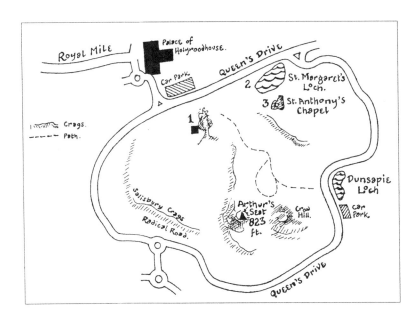

12
Three Other Walks to Explore

1 The Royal Botanical Garden
1 MILE NORTH OF CITY CENTRE
Bus: 8,9,23,27.
Car parking at Arboretum Place
OPEN 10AM TO 1 HOUR BEFORE SUNSET

The Royal Botanical Garden moved to Inverleith in 1823, and these 70 acres are mature and beautifully planned. The rock garden is delightful with its paths winding through the man made hills. There is also a heath garden, a woodland garden, a peat garden, a palm house and other exhibition houses. A guide to these is available at the gatehouse. There is also a visitor centre, **Inverleith House**. Watch out for the huge beech hedge, the orchid collection, the impressive six foot Victoria lily pads, and the squirrels...

2 Dirleton Castle
18 MILES EAST OF CITY CENTRE
Car: A1 then A198 past Gullane

Dirleton Castle is one of the most attractive castles in the area. 13th century in origin, the land was bought by the **De Vaux** family who built the original round tower with its immensely strong walls. This structure was extended from time to time, and in the 15th century the **Ruthven** family had the main Hall built as well as the classic Jacobean dwelling house. There is also a chapel and a prison, where in 1649 witches (both male and female) were held before being strangled and burned at the stake. The massive fortifications were to prove a successful deterrent until 1650, when the much improved fire power of the Cromwellian troops forced what was to be a final surrender. They left the castle a ruin.

Botanic Garden

81

Within the grounds is a bowling green, an herbaceous border which is superb in summer, and a fine **beehive dovecot**. The dovecot was built in the 16th century and had over a thousand nests.

A short walk from the castle is *YELLOWCRAIGS BEACH,* and an exceptionally pretty shoreline. 2 miles along the coast to the west is another notable East Lothian beach at *GULLANE,* one of the best beaches in Scotland.

3 Crichton Castle
A68 to Pathhead, then turn right for Crichton

Crichton Castle has played an important role in the history of Scotland. The tower is 14th century, but the rest dates from the 1580's when the castle was extended in the popular Italianate style. **Mary Queen of Scots** visited the castle 1562 to attend the marriage of her half brother to the Earl of Bothwell's sister. She later married Bothwell, a poor match and a disaster typical of her tragic life. Today, the dramatic ruins of Crichton Castle, standing alone on the desolate hillside, are an evocative reminder of these times.

The building which stands to one side of the castle is **the stable block**, with its horseshoe window. The buttresses were a later addition. In the village, **the kirk** dates from the 15th century when it was built by William Crichton, and it has been much altered over the years.

Crichton features in **Sir Walter Scott's** *Marmion,* and it was his disappointment about the castle's state of disrepair that led to its preservation.

Crichton Castle is open Mon-Sat 9.30-7pm, Sun 2-7pm in summer; winter weekends only, Sat 9.30-4pm, Sun 2-4pm.

It is possible to walk from Crichton to **Borthwick Castle**, which still bears the scars inflicted by Cromwell's cannons in 1650. Part of this cross country walk is along the old Edinburgh to Carlisle railway line, *the Waverley Route.*

"O what a tangled web we weave,
  When first we practise to deceive!"

Marmion by **Sir Walter Scott**

Notes

Notes

Notes